LIFE IN THE SHADOW
OF THE SWASTIKA

LIFE IN THE SHADOW
OF THE SWASTIKA

*An Incredible Story of Survival,
Bravery, and Renewal*

FRIEDA E. ROOS-VAN HESSEN

Harvest
Day
Books

Traverse City, Michigan

Life in the Shadow of the Swastika
An Incredible Story of Survival, Bravery, and Renewal
by Frieda Roos-van Hessen

Harvest Day Books

Published by Harvest Day Books, an imprint of
Book Marketing Solutions, LLC
10300 E. Leelanau Court
Traverse City, Michigan 49684
orders@BookMarketingSolutions.com
www.BookMarketingSolutions.com

Printed in the United States of America

Hessen, Frieda van.
    Life in the shadow of the swastika : an incredible story of survival,
bravery, and renewal / Frieda E. Roos-Van Hessen. -- Traverse City,
Mich. : Harvest Day Books, 2006.
        p. ; cm.
        ISBN-13: 978-0-9741345-8-1
        ISBN-10: 0-9741345-8-9
      1. Hessen, Frieda van. 2. Holocaust, Jewish (1939-1945)--
Personal narratives. 3. Sopranos (Singers)--Netherlands--
Biography. 4. Jewish women in the Holocaust--Netherlands--
Biography. 5. Holocaust, Jewish (1939-1945)--Netherlands--
Biography. 6. Women refugees--Biography. I. Title.

D804.5.W65 H47 2006
940.53/18092--dc22   0610

Unless otherwise noted, Scripture references are from the King James Version of the Bible. All family names are authentic; some other names have been changed in the interest of privacy.

This book is available at:
www.ReadingUp.com

DEDICATION

To my daughter, Felicia.

AUTHOR'S NOTE

One thing I want, more than anything else, is for future generations to be aware of the danger of anti-Semitism. To have that taught in schools would be a dream come true! I have always wanted my book to be considered a story of bravery rather than of despair, in the midst of the incredible circumstances of that time in history called World War II.

"I knew Him . . . I knew Him . . .
I just didn't know His name . . . "

— Helen Keller

The Netherlands

CONTENTS

ACKNOWLEDGEMENTS

I would like to acknowledge the following:

In memory of Uncle Koos, who insisted, after the War was over, that I write down my incredible war experiences so that others may benefit by it.

Chosen People Ministries, for the kind use of their facilities while writing this manuscript.

Eileen Miller, for her incredible patience and her assistance with this manuscript.

With gratitude,

Frieda E. Roos-van Hessen

Felicia

MY LETTER: *To Felicia*

Autumn 1949

Dearest Felicia,

Y ou are still a little girl. To grasp and to understand at your tender age the extreme anxieties, horrors, and sorrows that go with a war would be impossible. But later, darling, when you grow up, you may want to know what people like Mommy went through. How, with God's help, we did survive, and were able to start a new life again, live in the "New World," begat lovely children, and build a new generation — always hoping that this new generation shall use its intelligence for the enlightenment, rather than the destruction, of mankind.

I don't know what kind of a day it was when I was born. It must have been a day with blue skies and dark clouds with silver linings, behind which were blue skies again. This would justly symbolize my life as it turned out in the future — how God, in His mercy, saw me through the Holocaust, and how I found Jesus as my Messiah.

With love to you Felicia,
Mom

If the Lord had not been on our side, we would have been swallowed alive by our enemies. Blessed be Jehovah, who has not let them devour us. We have escaped with our lives. Our help is from the Lord.

Psalm 124, The Living Bible

BEFORE THE WAR:
Growing Up

M y child, before relating to you how God in His mercy saw me through the Holocaust, I want to tell you a little about my life, so that later you will know Frieda, your mom.

I was born Frieda Ella van Hessen on April 24, 1915 in Amsterdam, The Netherlands. We lived at 121 Nieuwe Herengracht, in Amsterdam. It was a big home built in the eighteenth century, in the so-called "golden age" of Holland. In those early days, that home consisted of some forty rooms, which were later converted into three large apartments. We lived on the top floor, which included a very large attic that we converted into guest rooms. We also occupied the full basement for business purposes.

During the war, our home was ransacked for wood to be used for heating purposes. People knew that all of the three-story building inhabitants were taken away or had left, and the house was turned into ruins, the stones taken from the structure and thrown on a "flat boat" in the canal. When I went back some time after the war to see where I had lived my splendid, carefree, and blessed life, there was a big gaping hole where the building once stood. I nearly collapsed at the sight. The wallpaper from my bedroom was somehow on the retaining wall of the next building; it reminded me of my golden days in that once-so-cherished home.

In the 1980s I returned again to Amsterdam. Where our big home once stood, two houses had been constructed, leaving me with just the memories. Looking over at the other side of the canal, I saw lovely Wertheim Park (so named after a famous philanthropic Jew). Its gorgeous trees had remained the same over the years. I remembered the wonderful view from our third-story apartment, looking out at that park as I was wont to do with the rain pelting against our large windows. The park was still there. It was still captivating. And I realized that while people may change things, God never changes.

Before the war, the atmosphere in our home was that of music, and art and family. My mother, Sarlina Diamant, had a lovely soprano voice, which she apparently inherited from her father, Eliezar Diamant, who was a member of the then-famous Apollo Choir. She herself had studied with the famous Anton Averkamp, one of the best teachers in those days. However, she never sang professionally, and when Bernard, Eddie, and I came along, her aspirations to become a professional performer definitely ended. Later, when we children were attending the Conservatoire for Music to become musicians ourselves, we enjoyed listening to her voice, which was still very lovely, indeed. I adored my dad, and, being the only girl—with an older and a younger brother — I was

"Daddy's little girl." My father was a businessman and captain of the Corps of Engineers with the Dutch Army Reserve. During the Dutch mobilization, he was asked to become a full-time officer.

As for a Jewish religious education, there was none for me. But my brothers both had a bar mitzvah and married in the synagogue. As a six-year-old child, when I asked why I had to stay home from school on "Grote Verzoendag" (the Day of Atonement), I was told that it was just another holiday. Christianity was never mentioned in our home either.

We had yearly family membership to the zoo, and the very earliest concerts we attended as a family — Mom and Dad, and my two brothers, Bernard and Eddie — were on Sunday afternoons in the big music tent. That really laid the foundation for my career as a classical singer, as well as our parents taking us to concerts and operas as we grew up. I used to love to go to the zoo, and it probably was the reason for my love of animals.

Entering the zoo, a long lane with all kinds of birds on both sides welcomed us. Perched outside their cages on poles, they were beautiful and noisy! Some were white and pink cockatoos with their cuffs standing up high, as they were doing what good cockatoos do — dancing up and down. There were also very large multi-colored parrots from South America, and many other kinds of birds in fascinating colors from all over the world. That must have been where I developed my interest in painting birds and creating needlepoint with their images years later. I just love colors, and I think they are a gift from God. Just look at the rainbow and the perfect colors He designed!

And then there was "het houtere gezicht van Sinterklaas" (the wooden face of St. Nicholas). This is a story about my little brother Eddie and myself that I think you will really enjoy. Eddie was about four years old and I about five (I was fourteen months older). One fine day, my mom decided that our older brother, Bernard, was to impersonate St. Nicholas for us younger children. This saint, we were told, came all the way from Spain in the middle ages to bring presents to the children in Holland after a time of war. Even to this day, this is a great event for the children. Sinterklaas arrives on a boat in Amsterdam's harbor with his helper, Black Pete. Dressed in his bright, red robe holding his golden scepter, Sinterklaas mounts a great white stallion and rides through the streets of Amsterdam with hundreds of people — mainly parents with their children — following him.

At the time, Bernard was about thirteen years old. Bernard was not tall, so we were told that he was "the son of Sinterklaas" because Sinterklaas was too busy to come himself since he was preparing for the long journey from Spain on December 5th, the official day of his arrival in Holland. Bernard played the role well. He wore a wooden mask that looked like the face of Sinterklaas, an old man with a long, white beard. We never surmised that it was our big brother, nor did we think it strange at the time that the son of St. Nicholas had a white beard! Afterwards, we told Bernard how sorry we were that he had to go on an errand for Mom, and that he had missed Santa's son, who had come to visit us. We then showed him the little presents he had brought us.

There were times after that visit, when we were naughty, that my mom would just show us that wooden mask around the door. Any problem with misbehavior was instantly solved because the thing scared us to death. As children, we were told that if we did not behave, we would not get any presents from Sinterklaas when he arrived from Spain. Now as I look back, the funniest part of it all was that the mask was kept in my parent's bedroom in a chest of drawers. Knowing about it, we were terrified to pass by that piece of furniture. We whispered "het houtere gezicht van Sinterklaas" is in that drawer, and though we knew it was made of wood, we walked very carefully around the chest just in case. We were scared that Sinterklaas mask would come out.

At the age of six, I went to "the big school" after attending kindergarten. My outgoing, impetuous, and playful nature was quite a shock to my teachers, causing me trouble all through my school years. They definitely had other plans for me. So, starting in elementary school, to make me behave, Mrs. Meyer, my first teacher, would take the yellow towel she used to clean the chalk off the big slate board in front of the class, fold it in a triangle, place it over my mouth, and knot it behind my head. She had it all figured out! This was a perfect way to stop Frieda from talking and joking. It was not the most sanitary way, but it worked, at least for a while. In high school, I sat all alone way in the back of the classroom so as not to disturb the others. Although my jolly and carefree attitude made me a problem for my teachers, I became very popular with my classmates, who always helped me out whenever I was in trouble.

There was a handcraft class for boys and one for girls. As a girl, I learned to knit, crochet, and embroider — all things I used later as an adult. Yet there was one thing I could not do, and that was sew on a sewing machine. In those days, sewing machines were totally manual, and you had to use a foot pedal to make the needle move up and down, while moving the cloth with your hands. It was too complicated for me, and, thanks to my popularity, all I had to do was ask one of the girls if she would please do it for me. They were always more than willing to comply. The only bad thing was that I never learned to sew on a machine. But look how the Lord has replenished that shortcoming, allowing me to create fine needlepoint and tapestries later on. What a blessing!!

Water sports are definitely included in bringing up children in Holland. At the age of nine, I went to the indoor swimming pool for the first time and began my lessons. I worked hard at it and loved it until I was to be tested in order to be awarded the diploma of an "accomplished swimmer." Instead of having me just get in the pool and swimming, they put an adult woman's very large corset on me. In those days, corsets had long bones in them to keep the body erect, and they covered just about half of your torso. The next thing I knew, they put big boots on my feet and then told me to jump into the water! This was to train me in case I fell into one of the canals so I would be prepared and able to survive. I earned extra points if I did well in saving the life of someone else that had fallen in. For that reason, they threw a big doll—all dressed and the size of an adult — in the water, and I had to "save its life." In Holland, we were well-prepared to save a life if necessary. Today, things are different. Amsterdam has a special unit to "fish" cars out of the canal, which seems to be a daily occurrence. We did not have to worry about such things in my youth. Life was so much simpler; we mostly rode bicycles!

Some years later, my dad was one of the first to own a car in Amsterdam. We were so proud of our American made Overland, which was also one of the first cars on the market in Holland. We had it for several years, until my dad decided he needed a change.

He bought a bright red "two-seater." Mom was horrified and told him, "the only thing missing is a copper bell so it can be used as a fire wagon!" But we kids loved it because a "two-seater" was a small convertible, and that was truly an attraction for us. Not only did we get a ride, but feeling the fresh air on our faces instead of smelling gasoline was, to us, a miracle. And it was a red car to boot!

There are many other stories to tell you of family and friends, of laughter and joy. But those will have to wait until another day. For now I must relate to you those tales that are most important, pertaining to my eight incredible escapes from the Nazis.

FOREBODING

I was "sweet sixteen" and had just finished high school. During the last year of school, every student had saved fifty cents a week for a trip outside of Holland. Finally, after a tough year of study, school was over, and it was time for summer vacation — and there was enough money for all of us to travel!

We had decided to go on a hiking trip and visit the beautiful mountains of Germany. Where we lived in Holland, the terrain was flat. Thus, we were an excited group of youth when we exited the train that day in Westphalia, a region in northwest Germany. With our hard work all finished, and the burden of years of education now behind us, we were ready for a wonderful adventure together.

All went well those first few days of the trip. The scenery was stupendous and enjoying it together was exhilarating. However one day, as our boisterous bunch was promenading through the city of Altena, a huge man stopped in his tracks in front of us. Suddenly, pointing his finger in my face, he shouted to my friends, "Is she Jewish?!!"

We were absolutely dumbfounded. The words came with such force that they took my breath away. In our young world in Holland, we knew nothing of religious or racial distinctions and differences, at least not to the extent that being Jewish was held against us. I remember how little redheaded Ann whispered to me to deny it. "They hate the Jews here!" she said. But the Dutch are a very stubborn and proud people, so I faced him, and boldly staring him in the face I declared, "Yes, sir, I am!" His face turned crimson with anger as he bellowed, "You'll find out soon what will happen to all of you rotten Jews!"

Then, glaring at me, he abruptly turned and stomped off, leaving all of us shocked and stunned. At that point, before Hitler's total dominance over Europe, we Dutch teenagers could not possibly have fathomed the calamity which was to befall us. It was as if the "voice of doom" had sounded, introducing us to the unholy reign of Nazism, which was soon to persecute the Jewish people.

Naturally, that incident took the fun out of our day and deflated our spirits, therefore we returned to the youth center. We girls went into the washroom to freshen up and noticed a small group of teenagers. They were much like ourselves, except they were German. Unexpectedly, one of them came over to me and asked if I was Jewish. Upset by the fact that this was the second time in one day that I was confronted with this same question, I looked straight into her eyes and blurted out, "Yes. So what?" Apparently she was not at all surprised at my reply and begged me not to be angry with her. "We are Christians," she explained, pointing to the other girls, "and we truly love the Jews. But," she said, "I am sad to say that many of our countrymen hate the Jewish people."

"Thank goodness," I thought to myself, "Hitler hasn't brainwashed everyone to hate the Jewish people!" We shared some small talk, leaving our new acquaintances when a bell rang announcing that it was supper time.

WHO WAS THIS? AN ANGEL?

"But thou and thy father's house shall be destroyed, and who knows whether thou art come to the kingdom for such a time as this?" Esther 4:14

On the very next day, as we were strolling through a small town, a gentleman dressed in a long, black coat, and wearing a black hat appeared. This gentleman came up to me and asked if I was Jewish. "Not again!" I thought to myself. I told him, "Yes." Holding out a black, leather-covered book, he begged me to accept it. It was, in his words, "the Word of God." He then implored me to "bitte lesen Sie Esther," which means, "please read the Book of Esther." I looked down at the book and when I looked up again, he was gone . . . Could he have been an angel of God, warning me of what was going to happen? Because he called the book "the Word of God," I was so afraid of it that I not only put it at the bottom of my suitcase, but once home, I put it at the very bottom of my music library. After all, this was "the Word of God" and I was scared to death of it. I am sad to say that I did not know Him then and it was years before I would read it. To this day, I do not know whether he was an angel of God, as the Scriptures tell us that, at times, we have "entertained angels unawares." (Hebrews 13:2)

The following day we walked to Hohelimburg, a small, lovely town with its youth center built right on top of a mountain. The fifteen-mile hike to the top was truly glorious. We sang all the way, while our eyes feasted themselves upon lovely sights: valleys laden with flowers; high hills with pine trees; a picturesque, little church; rare birds; and 1001 other things we thought were grand. However, it was an extremely hot day, and a change was brewing. Towards the end of our trip up the mountain, we noticed that dark grey clouds were gathering over us. Their little pink "heads" predicted an electrical storm. We knew it wouldn't be long before the storm broke, and we feared we would be caught in it before we reached the youth center.

Suddenly, a streak of lightning cut through the sky. The clouds opened up and poured out what seemed like their very last drop of rain upon us, and in no time we were soaked to the skin. There was nowhere to hide, and since we couldn't possibly get any wetter than we already were, our teacher decided that we would keep on walking, but at a faster pace, until we reached the youth hostel. Upon our boisterous arrival there, the manager and his good wife saw that we were soaked. They took wonderful care of us, not only seeing to it that our clothes were put up to dry, but immediately serving us bowls of delicious, hot soup so we would not get chilled.

In spite of the soup, I caught a bad cold and wasn't allowed to join the hike the following day. Instead, our teacher sent me on ahead by train to Freiburg, the next planned stop on our trip. Here, in the midst of magnificent mountains, a fifteenth-century castle had been converted into one of the most beautiful youth hostels you've ever seen. As magnificent as it was, I still felt so miserable that the only thing I wanted to do was go straight to bed . . . I sank into a deep sleep, out of which I awoke the next morning feeling so much better. I got dressed and went downstairs to explore the castle. After all, one doesn't get to live in an honest-to-goodness castle every day.

BALTHASAR

I bought some postcards in the castle's gift shop to send to my friends and family. As I was writing my greetings to them, a tall, good-looking, young, blond German man sauntered over to me and introduced himself. His name was Balthasar Streitle. After chatting a while with him, I found out that he was the son of the director of the electrical power plant in Luedenscheid, a town in Westphalia. After talking for a bit, Balthasar asked me for a date, and providing I felt well enough, we would go for a walk the next day. He seemed so nice, and I was really looking forward to spending some time with him.

Feeling much better the following morning, I met Balthasar for a delightful walk in the surrounding hills. We had such a wonderful time — an opportunity to talk in ideal surroundings. Everything seemed perfect, or so I thought. As we were climbing a hill, we noticed some people who were coming down. The path was rather narrow, and as they approached, Balthasar unexpectedly shoved me way over to the other side. After they passed, I asked him why he had pushed me like that. He said that those people's "political inclinations" were different, and he did not think it was "desirable" for me to get too close to them. I assumed he was protecting me from becoming contaminated. Well, Balthasar and I were out to have fun, so I put it out of my mind completely. The rest of the day was without incident, and together we returned to the castle rather happy.

The rest of my group arrived in Freiburg the next day. I didn't see much more of Balthasar because we students had to stay with our own group. However, I did have a chance to say goodbye to him, and we decided to write to each other. For me, the motivation was not only to improve my German, but also because I was really taken with him! I wrote to Balthasar as soon as my group returned to Holland, and for the subsequent six months I received the most charming letters back. Balthasar was a very sociable writer. How, then, can I describe my shock and dismay when one day I found in my mailbox a letter from him and a newspaper called *The Luedenscheider Beobachter* (The Luedenscheider Observer).

I opened it up, and there, right on the front page, was a picture of Balthasar—in full Nazi regalia! He was holding a gigantic swastika in his hand, and under his picture was written "Our New Nazi Youth Leader." Was this the sweet, young man with whom I had strolled the hills of Freiburg? The picture I now saw bore no resemblance to the person who had written such endearing letters to me.

I was completely stunned. Balthasar never once mentioned politics when he had written to me. But in his accompanying letter, Balthasar praised Hitler and wrote about how thankful he was to his fuehrer. He went so far as to say, "if anyone dared to say anything against my fuehrer, I will kill them!"

This time I answered Balthasar with a very short, terse note and risked being killed. I told him exactly what I thought of him and his fuehrer. I wrote that Hitler was nothing less than a warmonger and, to top it all off, I told Balthasar that I was Jewish! I obviously never heard from him again.

As the incident on the hill came back to me, I realized that those people, whose "political inclinations were different" must have been Jews. Balthasar didn't know I was Jewish; he was "protecting" me from my own people! I often wondered how Balthasar rationalized falling in love with a Jewish girl.

WORSENING CIRCUMSTANCES

Kees Diericks became my boyfriend after my trip to Germany. He and I were going steady, but my parents were not pleased. Kees was not Jewish, and my parents told me to forget him. Because we could not meet at home, and the Dutch weather was very fickle, we would seek shelter in Catholic churches, where we would hug and kiss like all young people in love. When we walked through a church, I was always struck by the expression on the face of Jesus as displayed in the paintings of the "seven stages of the cross." At that time, I did not realize that He suffered for all of us, Jew as well as Gentile.

In 1933, there was a growing Fascist regime in Italy and German Nazism was well on its way — the political situation in Europe became very tense. There had arisen in Holland a new political party, the N.S.B., or National Socialist Party. This group of Mussolini and Hitler followers was indoctrinating and brainwashing some of our young people into becoming Fascists.

One day I noticed that some of Kees' friends were trying to lure him into joining the N.S.B. He had mentioned this to me several times, but I had never taken him seriously. And at that time, I did not have the slightest idea of the extent of the disaster awaiting the Jewish people. Kees had become so angry with my parents for not letting us go steady, that when I came back from my trip to Germany, I found out he had joined the N.S.B.! Kees began openly wearing Fascist insignia and regularly attending their meetings. I explained to him how misguided he really was and tried in vain to stop him before he became too involved. But it was too late. Kees stubbornly refused to listen to my good advice. Unfortunately, he became more and more engulfed in Nazism. In the end, he paid for it with his very life, however not before destroying the lives of many innocent people, and almost mine as well.

The swastika was casting a dark shadow over not only Germany, but all of Europe. Its darkness would soon spread into every corner and touch every heart — some with its contamination, some with terror. The screaming man in the street, Balthasar, and Kees, had all been contaminated by its darkness. My friends, who already felt the icy fingers of fear, were immobilized from coming to my defense. Yet, in the center of this situation were bastions of light, like the Christian girls I had met. The trip to Germany was a turning point for me. The shadow, through these encounters with friends and strangers, had begun to cover me. But was the shadow that followed me for the next few years the shadow of the swastika, or was it the shadow of the Almighty? Time would tell.

A MUSICAL HOME

I must have inherited my love for music from my mother and her family. I was told that Grandpa Eli had a wonderful baritone voice, and the men's choir he sang with won many prizes at music festivals. My own mother also had a lovely soprano voice and studied with the famous Anton Averkamp, one of the best teachers in those days. However, she never sang professionally, and when Bernard, Eddie and I came along, her aspirations to become a professional performer definitely came to an end.

When I was about six years old, Eddie and I began our musical education. I started my piano lessons while Eddie, who wanted to learn to play the violin, was given the smallest violin you ever saw, the so-called quarter size. Bernard already played the piano beautifully. He was so talented that it served him well in later years when all of us became musicians and performed together, broadcasting and giving "house concerts." We were quite small when we first started our lessons, and Eddie in particular was very little. After our first year of study, we were to perform at a students' concert. When it was Eddie's turn to play, the audience had to wait because he had temporarlily disappeared behind the grand piano. He was so short that someone had to get a box for him to stand on, much to the amusement of the audience. "Good things come in small packages" they say, and Eddie, tiny in size, performed beautifully. Our parents' sacrifices for our education were well rewarded. Eddie became a very fine violinist growing up, until the holocaust cut his life short. Bernard became a fine pianist, and I a concert singer.

EVENT AT THE OPERA

I remember as if it were today. My mother had two tickets to the opera *Parsifal* by Richard Wagner, and I was chosen as the one to attend this performance with her because of my latent singing ability. I think I was about twelve years old. Now, *Parsifal* is a very heavy, very long opera, certainly for a twelve-year-old child. This was a Friday night performance, and I had been up early and in school all day. So I was not exactly what you would call "fit" to see and hear any opera, much less a long one. The performance didn't start until 8:00 p.m., and by the middle of the first act, I was struggling to stay awake. During the second act, I succumbed and finally dozed off. Apparently my mother had not noticed.

In the second act, Kundrie, one of the characters in the opera, emerges with a hideous shriek from the earth. That is, at least, what I remember seeing and hearing. This shriek was so intense, so loud, and so sudden, that I screamed, jumping straight out of my seat and screaming as loudly as Kundrie herself. This of course caused quite an uproar all around as people shushed and pointed at me. Needless to say, my mother wanted to be swallowed up by the earth as Kundrie had come out. I personally think a Wagner opera is too intense for a twelve-year-old child.

CAREER CHOICES

Once I was finished with my high school education, I began two paths of study. One would become not only my chosen profession but my life-long passion. I started a business course in secretarial education at Schoevers Business School, where I studied typing and stenography in the Dutch, English, French, and German languages. I finished the course in about two years, and at the age of seventeen, I accepted an offer to work at Lam's Wholesale Diamond Experts as a secretary. I had also reached the age where most voice teachers generally acknowledge the voice has stabilized and will no longer change. My parents decided that now was the time to begin my voice lessons, which was the true desire of my heart. So while working as a secretary at Lams, I also embarked on my future career as a concert performer. The foundation was laid at the Amsterdam Conservatoire for Music. I practiced my vocalizations early every morning before going to work, then at lunchtime I either went to a singing lesson or one in music theory, and at night I completed other required subjects.

After a while, the managers of the Lam Company insisted that I also learn about the quality and details of the diamonds. The president of the firm, Mr. Lam, was a man in his sixties, who always dressed very chic wearing a carnation in his lapel. One day, upon returning from my lesson at lunchtime, my supervisor, Karl, was waiting for me at the elevator. He told me that Mr. Lam had been on the floor, on his knees, for over an hour, carnation and all, picking up the diamonds I had apparently thrown on the floor when I banged my fist on the table each time I lost count. They were tiny, little things I was supposed to place into piles of one hundred by first counting them out ten at a time. I don't know how many times I got lost in the count. All I remembered at the time Karl confronted me was that I had lost my temper.

Karl suggested that I resign from my position because it became evident to both of us that I was not meant to become a technician in the diamond field. I spoke with my parents about this and we felt the time had come for me to put all my efforts into studying music and my upcoming exams. I went to speak with the office manager and asked to be relieved of my job. She did not have to think about it twice and wholeheartedly agreed that the diamond business was not exactly my calling. Receiving her best wishes, along with a very good letter of recommendation, I left my job, which was the last job I held in an office for many years.

I studied my music very seriously, passed my exams, and was accepted as a full-time student at the Amsterdam Conservatoire for Music. At the Conservatoire, I studied voice with Rose Schoenberg and attended the opera class to learn to act and sing. The opera class gave students a chance to do volunteer work on the stage of the Amsterdam Opera. My very first steps on the stage turned out to be very precarious. Pierre Monteux was the conductor of Bizet's *Carmen*, and I was chosen to be one of the "cigarette girls" in the first act. Much to my great joy, and ego, I was to walk from one end of the stage to the other, all by myself! What an opportunity and what an incredible moment that was going to be! The dress rehearsal was on Friday night, and as usual, it was sold out, even though it was not yet the official performance. The time came for our little group to sing, and I was to cross over from one end of the stage to the other. I started walking slowly, enjoying the fact that all eyes were on me. Then, when I got to exactly the middle of the stage, my one foot got caught in the very long skirt I was wearing, and before I knew it, I, in all my glory, was lying on the floor. Mr. Monteux had a fit, and looking at me with disgust, kept going as if "there never was a girl named Frieda."

On another occasion, we performed *the Rosenkavalier* by Richard Strauss. In the second act, one of the girls was standing so close to the lit candles that her wig caught fire and they had to throw water over her head to avoid a disaster. So you see, my dear Felicia, becoming an opera star is not that easy!

CONCERT CAREER

Some time later, one of Holland's broadcasting companies offered my teacher, Rose Schoenberg, a broadcasting time for a Sunday night concert. She was to choose her best students to sing during that hour, and the broadcasting company would pay for the radio time. This was a tremendous break for all of us. Although I had only studied with her for about a year-and-a-half, Madame Schoenberg chose me to sing the lovely aria by Blonde, from Mozart's opera, *The Seraillo*, the "Bell Song" from the opera *Lakmé* by Delíbes, and the soprano part in a trio from Bach's *Magnificat*. That was my first of many live radio broadcasts, and to this day I still remember how nervous I was. But it was such a wonderful opportunity for me.

As it turned out, the entire hour went extemely well, making our teacher very proud of us all. To my great surprise, I received a contract in the mail a few days later to sing the part of Mimi in *La Boheme*. One was technically not allowed to perform while still enrolled at the Conservatoire, but my teacher arranged for me to be able to accept this offer in spite of the school's regulation. My singing career had officially begun!

In the meantime, Walt Disney's *Snow White* film was released in America, and the company was looking for a Dutch Snow White to sing the role for a Dutch version of the movie. As usual, the Lord had it all prepared for me. Madame Schoenberg was to hold one of her famous pupil concerts again, and I was to perform the famous "Bell Song" from the opera *Lakme* by Delibes. When the performance came to an end, a gentleman by the name of Max Tak approached me. He had been a conductor in a movie theatre before the movies had sound. Mr. Tak's conducting services were no longer needed since the 'talking' movies had come out, and he had become a music critic for one of the more prominent newspapers in Holland. Madam Schoenberg had invited him to our concert to report on her success. When he heard me sing, he invited me to meet with him and Kurt Gerron, the famous filmmaker in Germany, who had been contracted to make the European versions of the Disney film. I was hired for the part of Snow White in the Dutch version, which is still being played today for the children during their summer vacation time. It was voted the best musical version in Europe, which softened the blow of my earlier *Carmen* disaster.

Thus was my career launched. The highlights, in those early days, were: a performance of Verdi's *Requiem* (of which I sang the soprano part) for the Dutch royal family; winning the Grande Diplome at the World Contest in Geneva; an engagement to sing the role of Waldvogel in Wagner's *Siegfried*, performed in Amsterdam by the Bayreuth Festspielhaus Opera Company and conducted by the late, world-famous conductor, Erich Kleiber, in a guest performance under the auspices of the Wagner Society in Amsterdam; and performances in the role of the Queen of the Night, in Mozart's *The Magic Flute*, also for the Wagner Society of Amsterdam. There were many radio broadcast concerts with the Radio Philharmonic Orchestra and other symphony orchestras, as well as a lieder recital with piano accompaniment in Amsterdam's Concertgebouw (the equivalent of New York's Carnegie Hall), as the prize for winning the Music Performance Contest of Holland.

At that point, Europe changed as World War II broke out, and this wonderful life of ours came to an end. The Holocaust destroyed 6,000,000 of our people, including most of your family, my dearest Felicia. Praise God, I survived!

From the monthly "Radio Guide" which was in wide circulation throughout The Netherlands.

Translation of caption: "The Radio Orchestra directed by Albert van Raalte. Soloist Frieda van Hessen."

Another concert date featuring Frieda van Hessen, from the monthly Radio Guide.

(3.45)   Voor de kleintjes
„Leloe is thuis
in het nieuwe huis"
Een verhaal in stukken van
H. Wolffenbüttel-van Rooyen
XVI

(4.00)   De Vrolijke Klas

HILVERSUM

Golflengte 1875 m.   (160 k.p.)
en 301.5 m.   (995 k.p.)

V. A. R. A.

8.00 Tijdsein

8.01   AAN DE STRIJDERS
(Altijk
(grammofoonmuziek)

8.05   ESMERALDA
o.l.v.
Eddy Walis

(8.15 Morse-tijdsein)
±8.16 Buitenlands weersverzicht
en weersverwachting

8.30   GRAMMOFOONMUZIEK

9.30   ONZE KEUKEN
door
P. J. Kers Jr.

V. P. R. O.

10.00 Morgenwijding
Voorganger: Ds. J. P. C. Poldervaart

V. A. R. A.

10.20   UITZENDING
VOOR DE ARBEIDERS IN
DE CONTINU-BEDRIJVEN

De strijd tegen
ziekte en dood
Een viertal lezingen
te houden door
Dr. H. Peeters
I
„De betekenis van Röntgenstralen
voor de geneeskunst"
(Herhaling van de uitzending op
Vrijdag 13 Januari j.l.)

(10.40) Tilly Perin-Bouwmeester
en
Wim Kan
in een liedje en een praatje
„Zo zijn de vrouwen!"
Aan de vleugel:
Daaf Wins

R. V. U.

11.00 „De Hond", hoe men hem voedt,
verzorgt en maatschappelijk maakt.
Cursus van P. M. C. Toepoel, schrij-
ver van diverse boeken over de hond
en keurmeester te Laren.

V. A. R. A.

11.30   GRAMMOFOONMUZIEK
Fantasie „Rip van Winkle"
Planquette
Symphonie-orkest o.l.v.
Manfred Gurlitt

11.40   UITZENDING
VOOR DE WERKLOZEN
Andries Sternheim spreekt over:
„Werkloosheidsbestrijding in
het buitenland"

12.00 Tijdsein

12.01   GRAMMOFOONMUZIEK
(±12.15 Buitenlands weersverzicht
en weersverwachting)
1. Posthoorn-galop
Koenig-Mortimer
Foden's Motor Works Band
o.l.v. H. Mortimer

43

8.21   Film over het leven van Joh. Strauss   8.50

DE ONSTERFELIJKE

2. Ta-hu-wa-hu-wa-i   Noble
Andy Iona and His Islanders
3. Tin Pan Alley medley no. 8
Ivor Moreton en Dave Kaye,
piano-duet, met bas en slagwerk
4. Alexander's ragtime band
memories
Hildegarde met beg. van twee
piano's, bas en guitaar
5. De acrobaat (dans-intermezzo)
Orkest Paul Godwin   Robrecht
6. Mussenparade (karakterstukje)
Rathke
Orkest o.l.v. Franz Alfred Schmidt
7. Täubchen, das entflattert ist
(uit: „Die Fledermaus")
Genée-Haffner-Strauss
Marcel Wittrisch en Anni Frind
met orkestbeg.
8. Mariska (lied en czardas) Lehár
Lajos Kiss en zijn orkest

12.30   COR STEYN
bespeelt het orgel van het
City-Theater te Amsterdam
1. Künstlerpech (ouverture)
Armandola
2. Heimlichkeiten   Rust
3. Habanera   Algra
4. Choir Boy   Arnold
5. Der Zarewitch (fantasie)   Lehár

1.00   VARA-ORKEST
o.l.v.
Hugo de Groot
m.m.v.
Frieda van Hessen
coloratuur-zangeres

1. Joyeuse marche   Chabrier
2. a. Berceuse   Järnefelt
b. Preludium   Järnefelt
3. a. Die Nachtigall   Alabief
b. Il Bacio   Arditi
(zang en orkest)
4. Balletmuziek uit de opera „Die
verkaufte Braut"   Smetana
a. polka
b. furiant
c. danse des comédients
5. Cavatine (Una voce poco vá)
(uit de opera „De barbier van
Sevilla")   Rossini
(zang en orkest)
6. Ouverture der opera „De macht
van het noodlot"   Verdi

*FRIEDA VAN HESSEN,
coloratuur-zangeres, werkt mede aan
het concert, dat het V.A.R.A.-Orkest
van 1.00—1.45 geeft o.l.v.
Hugo de Groot*

1.45 Onderbreking voor ver-
zorging van de zender

2.00 Tijdsein

2.01   VOOR DE VROUWEN
Programma:
VARA-Knipcursus
o.l.v.
Miep Olff-van Boven
(beginners)
negentiende les

(2.25) Grammofoonmuziek
Wals uit het ballet „Coppelia"
Mark Hambourg, piano   Delibes

(2.30) Gesprekken met vrouwen
„Wat ons verenigt"
(Een woord tot de vrouwen op het
platteland)
Toespraak te houden door
Mevr. A. J. Aarsen-Jansen
(Uitzending in samenwerking met
de Bond van Soc. Democratische
Vrouwenclubs)

(2.50) Overschakelen naar
de versterkte zender

(2.55) VARA-Knipcursus
o.l.v.
Miep Olff-van Boven
(gevorderden)
negentiende les

(3.15 Morse-tijdsein)

3.15   VOOR DE KINDEREN
Programma:
Kinderzang klinkt in de huiskamer!
Zangles door
„De Roodborstjes"
o.l.v.
Henk van Laar

*ANDRIES STERNHEIM
spreekt om 11.40 v.m. over de werkloosheidsbestrijding in het buitenland*

41

Advertisement in *The Jewish Weekly* during wartime. The advertisement was similar to a giant billboard which was prominently displayed on the side of the Theater van de Lach where Frieda performed (indicated by arrow).

THE INVASION:
The Last Train

Although my personal life was flourishing, a storm was brewing in Europe. With the advancing growth of Hitler's German Nazi party, the European political situation was becoming worse. It finally became so bad that, because of the threat of war, the Dutch army was mobilized. My dad, an Army Reserve officer carrying the rank of captain of the Corps of Engineers, became a commanding officer of the regiment in and around the city of Gouda. Because of its nearness to the Merwede Canal, Gouda was a city of high strategic value and vital to the defense of the provinces of Zeeland, South Holland, and North Holland.

On May 8, 1940, I was to give a concert in Enschede in the province of Overysel, which directly bordered on Germany's Westphalia. Halfway through the concert, we heard the rapid-fire shooting of borderline conflict, and we all knew that real trouble was not far off. But, in spite of everyone's uneasiness, I was asked to sing several more encores, with much success.

I was scheduled to return the following day, but when I arrived at the train station, I was told that there wouldn't be any more trains until further notice. We heard all kinds of rumors, and then suddenly the news spread like lightening: "The queen has declared that the Kingdom of The Netherlands is in the state of emergency!" Eventually I was told that there might be one more train going west, which, as it turned out, would be the last one for a long time to come.

I waited all that day, and finally, at 5:00 p.m., the last train was scheduled to depart from the station. Everyone got on, and slowly the overloaded train lumbered toward Amsterdam. We began to cross the giant bridge over the River Maas. A beautiful bridge it was, long and strong. No sooner had we crossed the bridge, we were overtaken by a deafening roar. In order to protect the western part of our country from attack by the Germans, our army engineers had blown up the bridge after our train had passed to prevent it from being used as a point of entry. No wonder we were told this would be "the last train for a long time to come!"

No bridge, no traffic, no trains. My dad, being an officer, of course knew how much real trouble we were in. He called my mother from his post in Gouda, urging her to get me back home as soon as she could. But it was already impossible to make phone calls to those remote places where I had been singing. Naturally, everyone at home was panic-stricken, and my mother in tears when she couldn't even reach me by phone. What joy and excitement when, very late that night, I arrived safely home. They asked me a thousand questions, and I had so much to tell them that time simply seemed to fly. It was past midnight when we all went to bed, exhausted from tension and excitement. I fell into a deep sleep, unaware of the dark clouds that were gathering over our heads.

WAR

I was awakened by someone grabbing me by the arm and shaking me while shouting. Jerked out of my deep sleep, it was my brother Bernard who was frantically screaming at me: "We are in war! There is war! The Germans are attacking us! We are at war!"

"War?!" I jumped out of bed. Clearly awake now, I ran to the windows where the rest of the family was already scanning the skies. I saw the German bombers — those horrible, black monsters with white swastikas painted underneath — looking like huge birds of prey as they swept right over our rooftops, Our house was directly situated in their route to Schiphol, our airport. Suddenly, we heard the eerie screams of the bombs as they were released and the tremendous roar as they exploded. This was Holland's first great bombardment. As I watched in horror, I remembered my dream of six months earlier, in which I had seen gigantic black birds flying straight over our house. At that time, I wondered what it meant. Now I knew.

The radio newscaster announced that Germany had made a surprise attack on Amsterdam's Schiphol Airport, the home of KLM Royal Dutch Airlines. After the Germans bombed it to pieces, it became impossible for the Dutch army to convert the commercial airport into a military facility.

The noise of the bombing was both terrifying and deafening, and our fear of what might happen next increased by the minute. We raced to the basement for shelter and stayed there for what seemed like an eternity. Finally, at dawn, when the bombing had stopped, we emerged, and the only thing we could think of or say was the word "radio." Just as quickly as we had all run to the basement, each of us tried to get upstairs before the others. We ran up three flights to hear the latest news. We clung to the radio, as if that poor thing could somehow erase the fact that the Nazis were overrunning our beautiful country. To our utter dismay, the newscaster said, "We are now officially at war with Germany."

I felt sick to my stomach. What about Dad? And what about my brother, Eddie? He was in the army, too. Would we ever see them again? No one knew.

PANIC AMONG THE JEWS

"They're going to kill the Jews! Let's get out of the country before it's too late!" We were overcome with panic just as suddenly as the bombers had appeared. Having already heard about the infamous "Crystal Night" — when the Nazis attacked Jewish citizens and stores in Germany — we knew we had to escape. Jewish people by the thousands left for Ymuiden, the small seaport on the North Sea, hoping to catch a freighter or fishing boat to England. Many did, but unfortunately, many more did not. Terrified for their lives, and having nowhere else to turn, many Jewish people took their own lives.

All we could think of was that we too, somehow, had to escape. Mother, Bernard, and I frantically packed our suitcases, throwing into them only those things we would need most. But, by the time our suitcases were ready, Mother tearfully declared that she could not possibly leave without Dad and Eddie. Deep down inside, we all felt the same way. We unpacked and waited for some word from Dad.

THE BATTLE FOR THE MERWEDEBRIDGE

Although it sounds impossible, Holland lost her war against Germany in four days. Dutch soldiers who, unbeknown to the military, were collaborators with the N.S.B. Fascist party, had betrayed our country to such an extent that the fight was over before it had begun. The story of the Merwedebridge is a classic of betrayal and undermining a defending army.

Our Merwedebridge was a masterpiece of construction and craftsmanship. It was one of the most strategic strongholds in all of southwestern Holland. The bridge is extremely long, indeed. This made it very difficult to know exactly what was happening on the other side. Our boys were fiercely defending this stronghold, knowing that their very lives depended on saving it. Without warning, our men noticed a regiment in Dutch uniform approaching from the other side. They thought the Germans had lost, and that these Dutch soldiers were coming to relieve them. By the time they realized this could never be our Army — coming from the other side — it was too late! Wearing Dutch uniforms, the Nazis had tricked our boys, and were now firing at them from close range, killing them, and thus winning the battle for the Merwedebridge.

Our surviving Dutch soldiers were taken captive and deported to POW camps in Germany. Later it was discovered that the N.S.B. had offered big army contracts, at a tremendous profit, to Fascist-minded textile manufacturers. These manufacturers, in turn, delivered Dutch uniforms to the Germans. With the aim of becoming the most powerful leader of greater Europe, Hitler had followers in all of Germany's neighboring countries, and by infiltrating their military, he succeeded in overthrowing those countries.

ROTTERDAM — THE BIG BOMBARDMENT

But the worst thing, by far, was the ruthless bombing of the city of Rotterdam. Rotterdam had been declared an "open city" because of the many hospitals and the Red Cross headquarters located there. According to international agreements, such open cities were considered protected areas and were not to be bombed. The Nazis, however, did not care much about international agreements, and flew their bombers right through the streets, killing men, women, and children by the thousands, and destroying three quarters of the city within little more than one hour's time. Not only were many people killed by bombs, many were mutilated by falling debris. Countless more were wounded. The Nazis, knowing the psychological effect this would have on the Dutch people, sent an ultimatum to our government. They demanded the complete surrender of all of our Armed Forces, or else the cities of Amsterdam and The Hague would be obliterated next.

THE RIVER YSEL

Meanwhile, a terrible battle was being fought at the River Ysel, a natural boundary between Holland's eastern and western provinces. Up to that point, the River Ysel kept the warring armies apart. But now, a fierce, long battle ensued. It has been estimated that the Germans lost more than 100,000 men in that battle. They continuously shipped soldiers in little rubber floats from one side of the river to the other; never stopping, they kept sending more men. Thousands were shot by our boys, and one after another they tumbled into the river. Finally, after hours of constant shooting, our canons and rifles became red hot. Our men kept up the fight as long as possible, but in the end, it was the canons, and rifles, and machine guns that failed them. The final result was our surrender.

My brother, Eddie, fought in that battle. Again, betrayal and infiltration by the enemy was the cause of much bloodshed and loss of life. When Eddie came home unexpectedly, he looked like a ghost. He broke down and wept bitterly, repeating one phrase over and over: "We were betrayed! We were betrayed!" Later he told us, "The Germans knew everything except my name." Here too, a major battle was lost due to betrayal.

THE ROYAL FAMILY ESCAPES

At the same time, the Nazis were trying to capture the Dutch royal family. The personal adjutant of Prince Bernhard was a German, for the convenience of the Prince, who was German by birth. The Prince had uncovered a plot to "either kill, or deport alive the entire royal family." He promptly shot this adjutant, and immediately accomplished a near miracle. He personally rushed Queen Wilhelmina, Princess Juliana (his wife), and their children aboard a submarine and safely escaped to England. But this flight of the royal family had an ill effect on our fighting men: It broke their resistance. One could hear the cry of lost hope everywhere. "What's the use of fighting now? The queen is gone. We're fighting for a lost cause."

Little did the Dutch people understand, let alone grasp, the courage and above all, the wisdom of this very difficult, yet all-important decision our queen had to make. Queen Wilhelmina and Prince Bernhard headed the Dutch Underground from England for the next four years. The queen, one of the wealthiest monarchs in the world, was able to financially assist the Allied forces in their battle for freedom. Had she remained in Holland, she probably would have been deported, or become a prisoner of war like Belgium's King Leopold — a prisoner in his own country. Because she had attended the synagogue in Amsterdam at least once a year, the Nazis resented her love for the Jewish people, even sarcastically calling her "The Queen of the Jews." According to the plot discovered by the prince, Queen Wilhelmina most likely would have been shot, had she been captured.

Holland was torn to pieces, our soldiers were disheartened, the Jewish people were panic-stricken, the future was unknown, and daily life was turning into a veritable hell. Such were the circumstances under which the so-called "victorious" German Occupation army entered our cities and towns. One could see no more than a handful of N.S.B. fanatics welcoming them. Newspapers carried pictures of women handing flowers to German soldiers, but of course everyone knew this was propaganda. The majority of our people were so bitter and sick at heart that they went as far as shutting their blinds when the Nazis marched through the streets. The Nazis understood this insult perfectly well, and they carried a permanent hatred for us in their hearts. But no matter how hard they tried, how many of our loved ones they killed, how much they robbed us or plundered our possessions or food, or how much they tried to dishearten us, they could not change our stubborn, defiant attitude.

INTRODUCTION TO DISASTER

As the Nazis began their persecution of Holland's Jewish population, my career as a concert artist naturally became more difficult. I had been scheduled to appear as guest soloist for the famous, all-male choir Apollo, and that concert was to take place one month later in Amsterdam's world famous Concertgebouw — the equivalent of America's Carnegie Hall. It was to be my first performance there, and we had all been greatly anticipating this event. It was a magnificent concert, indeed, followed by standing ovations and flowers. The next day, however, brought the first sign of what would happen to Jewish performers like me. All of the concert reviews in the daily papers were positive, except for one. It read: "Since we have suffered so much at the hands of the Jews, and since both the soloist and her accompanist are of the Jewish race, which we detest so immensely, I do not wish to review that part of the otherwise excellent concert of the Apollo choir . . ."

TONY

Around the same time, and after countless arguments about Fascism and Nazism, I finally broke off my relationship with Kees. Shortly afterward, however, I was introduced to Tony Dresden. His father, Sem Dresden, was the director of Amsterdam's Conservatoire for Music. After dating Tony for a while, I fell in love with him. Tony was an accomplished pianist, and I invited him to accompany me at that Apollo concert. The critic apparently was not aware that Tony was only half Jewish (his mother was Gentile) or else he would not have made such a statement. Tony and I actually planned to be married in the near future.

THE BIG LIE

The Nazis had successfully desensitized our government, and officially declared that Holland "would be left in peace and no harm done to anyone." This, of course, was diplomatic propaganda so we would not be overly suspicious and would be more likely to accept their rules, which were slowly, and I might say very fluidly, imposed upon us. After only a few months, the Nazis announced that, "for security reasons," everyone in the country had to be "registered."

The Nazis designed the now infamous Registration Card, which was truly one of the most devious devices ever fabricated. However, people can easily be deceived, and with some smooth propaganda over the radio, and articles in the daily papers, we too were soundly led astray. On certain appointed days, we all were to stand in line, like sheep, to wait for a little card which would later become the avenue to kill thousands of our Jewish people. They were handing us the card "for free." We had to supply two passport photos, one for their files and one to be pasted onto the card. Not only did everyone have to answer a lot of questions, but those questions included information about our religious affiliation. In this way, they could determine who was Jewish and who was not! This information, along with a photo, resulted in a death trap for 120,000 Jewish Dutch people, whose only crime was being born Jewish!!! If only we had known, I am sure no one would have cooperated with this heinous plan, at least not through their own free will.

It took three to four months for every person in Holland to be registered. During that period, everything was quiet — too quiet. One could almost feel something brewing in the air.

THE STAR OF DAVID FOR THE JEWS

No sooner had the "registration" been accomplished, a new regulation was imposed: All the Jews in Holland had to wear the Star of David. Made of fabric, some four inches in diameter, the star had to be sown visibly onto all our outer clothing. The colors were the same as those used during the Middle Ages to warn people of The Plague — a yellow background with a black Star of David. And in the middle, in bold, black letters, was the word *Jood*, meaning Jew.

My dear Felicia, I am sure you may never understand the tragic effect this had upon all of us. It was meant to be a stigma, and even though we Jews fought our emotions, we could not help be embarrassed. We felt very awkward, as though we were being branded as convicts. Every garment was ruined by that big yellow star with the word JEW in capital letters in the middle of it. It was designed to single us out. The star became a constant symbol of something heretofore unknown in our country — anti-Semitism. Up to that point, no one in our country considered us "a race apart"; we were all Dutch!

In spite of the stigma associated with wearing "the star," many Christians, including clergymen, obtained stars illegally via the Underground and sewed them onto their coats as a gesture of protest against the Nazis' latest regulation. When the Nazis discovered this display of sympathy, they plastered posters throughout the land, warning that any non-Jew caught wearing the Star of David would be considered a traitor and punished accordingly.

PERSECUTION OF JEWISH ARTISTS

By this time, all Jewish musicians and artists had been dismissed from whatever positions they filled. The world famous Concertgebouw Orchestra liquidated all its Jewish players when Willem Mengelberg, its equally-famous conductor, turned Nazi. He became best friends with Seys Inquart, the "commander in chief of the German occupation forces in The Netherlands." Mengelberg, German by birth, suddenly forgot all the Jewish philanthropists who had for years financed the orchestra. But even more sadly, he also forgot the many fine Jewish musicians who had bestowed their talent to make the Amsterdam Concertgebouw Orchestra one of the finest orchestras in the world. Of course, when the war was over, Mengelberg was exiled from Holland, and until the day he died he was forbidden to ever enter it freely again. He died in exile in Switzerland.

JEWISH THEATRES

For a singer like me, engagements were out of the question, except for those in the newly established "Jewish theatres." There were two theatres near the Jewish section of Amsterdam where Jewish artists were still allowed to perform. As a result of the persecution of the Jews in Europe, some of Germany's and Austria's finest artists had fled to Holland. In Amsterdam, they formed the "Theater der Prominenten," or the Theatre of the Prominents. Great performers like Max Ehrlich, Otto Aurich, Franz Engel, and Hans Steiner tried to make a living under those very unfortunate and miserable conditions. After the war, I learned that many of them, as well as the rest of the ensemble, were killed in concentration camps. Every one, except for Aurich, Steiner, and myself.

My engagement with the Theatre of the Prominents called for several arias and songs from my own repertoire, as well as acting in some German sketches which these great artists wrote themselves. I spoke German fluently, which proved to be of immeasurable value later, when I was in real life-threatening danger.

Performances were always sold out and the theatre packed, as this was now the only entertainment outlet for the Jewish people. Each show was a tremendous hit. But, this success would not last for very long.

CONTINUING PERSECUTION

With people starving in Germany, the Nazis confiscated and shipped most of Holland's food supply there. The stock of dried goods alone was estimated to have lasted at least for five years, so you can imagine how greedily the Nazis grabbed this all up. Trainloads of food simply disappeared from Holland. The Nazis stole almost everything we had — including our cattle — and left us with just enough so we would not die right away, but rather, slowly languish from starvation.

The Nazis then imposed their new Ration Card system upon us. Nothing could be obtained without the Ration Card. And in order to have a card, one needed to report to the proper office with their official Registration Card. This would prove near impossible as Jewish people went into hiding. As if the torment was not enough, all coal and fuel for heating and cooling was withheld from all Jewish institutions. This included Jewish hospitals, Jewish rest homes, and of course, the Jewish theatres.

THE EXTREME WINTER OF 1941

Winters in Holland are usually mild, but in 1941 nature played a sinister trick, and we had one of the severest winters Holland had ever experienced. Intense cold winds blew down from the north, and performing, singing, and playing in a frozen theatre was sheer torture. The owner of the Jewish theatre was a Nazi collaborator and rented the space to us only because there was money to be made in it. Being a close friend of the German commander in charge of Amsterdam, the owner was one of the first to impose the new rule of "no heat for Jews" upon us — his tenants!

Our theatre contract called for a certain number of performances, and as far as the owner was concerned, whether we liked it or not and whether we froze or not, we had to go "on with the show." There were times when he forced us to play for a handful of people who only came in that terribly cold weather because they felt so sorry for us. Those dear people covered themselves with blankets in an effort to stay warm. We were told that if we decided not to perform, we would be sued. You can well imagine who would win in such a lawsuit.

My appearances called for five costume changes, from one evening gown to the next. In rooms where the water pipes were frozen, the wind raged through broken windows, and small patches of water had turned into ice on the floors and hallways, one does not need much imagination to know what we went through. Since only Jews were playing at the theatre, no one took the trouble to make repairs to the building. I might as well have made my costume changes in the street.

RAZZIAS AT PASSOVER

We artists were suffering—not only from the freezing temperatures, but like every Jew, we lived literally in constant torment. We had a premonition that even worse things were to come upon us . . . It was as if a ferocious animal was pursuing us "before the kill." Then suddenly, there it was — "Razzia!!" Razzia means a plundering raid or military attack. My people were raided, dragged from their homes, and plundered, in addition to being grabbed right off the streets. All were shipped in cattle cars straight to concentration camps.

The Nazis always timed their attacks perfectly. They were well thought out for the greatest intimidating psychological effect. The first country wide "razzia" was held on our Jewish Passover in 1942. Many of the Jewish people had retreated to hotels in the country to celebrate the holiday. The Jews had celebrated Passover for over 5,000 years under God's holy reign, before the fuehrer began his unholy reign. That year, my fiancé, Tony, and I were invited to go to one of the smaller country hotels with my cousin Esther.

That year, the Jewish people were celebrating the Passover with very heavy hearts. Thousands were saying Kaddish, the traditional prayer for those who died. Many of their loved ones had committed suicide rather than be caught by the Nazis. All of us were weary and sad, and very pessimistic regarding our future.

While this mournful Passover was being "celebrated," the Nazis produced their devilish plan: They raided our synagogues and our hotels, large and small, capturing every person of Jewish descent they could find. The reality of our pending destruction, as a result of the razzias, set off an alarm in the hearts of all Jewish people in the land. Paralyzed by fear, our own tiny group hoped to God that somehow this would be a real Passover for us, that the Nazis would somehow "pass over" our small hotel. Maybe just because it was so small, the miracle of God happened — the Nazis did not come for us! At least for now, we were safe.

But, in Amsterdam, with its more than 80,000 Jewish inhabitants, the Nazis had the utmost opportunity to display their cruel intent. When the raid was over, we realized our preservation was miraculous, and we could think of only one thing — our relatives at home. Were they still alive? Were they still there? We had to get back to Amsterdam as soon as possible, so we packed and left immediately.

THE HEARTBREAK

In the midst of all our fear, heartbreak, and confusion, my fiancé, Tony, refused to go back to Amsterdam with me. He lived in The Hague, and told me plainly that he was not going to risk his life in Amsterdam for me. Tony was going home. His love for me apparently was not strong enough to share "until death do us part." His argument was that though his father, Sem Dresden was Jewish, he had a Gentile mother, so he was therefore free from the Nazis' threats upon his life. But, if he married me, he would be considered Jewish also, and subject to the same persecution we were enduring. In fact, this became the very reason his family coerced him into breaking off our engagement.

Shortly afterwards, I was visiting Tony at his home in The Hague, and a cousin asked me to go upstairs and meet with her in a room. There she informed me, in a businesslike way, that I should consider the engagement annulled and that there would be no marriage. I was then threatened: If I should decide to still pursue marriage, they would call the police. The coward he apparently was, Tony did not even dare to face me personally. I was not only brokenhearted, but even more, I was terribly insulted and embarrassed. I cried so much I found myself unable to sing for a long time. Not even one note would come out! And each time I tried, I burst out crying instead. I was truly devastated.

MIEKA

Several weeks later, I was approached by a group of Jewish performers who asked me to sing the lead role in Emmerich Kalmann's operetta *Countess Maritza*. I thought I needed time to consider it. But then, it not only afforded me the opportunity to try an unknown field (up to that time I had performed strictly in classical concert and opera work), even more so, it was a remedy for my painfully broken heart. To forget my grief, I accepted and signed the contract.

It was during one of the rehearsals of *Maritza* that I met Mieka. She would be my best friend for years to come, and was apparently destined to be the one person to share with me the slowly but ever more closely approaching tragedy of our personal persecution. Mieka's sister, Andrea, one of our ballerinas, introduced us. After this first meeting, I was invited to Mieka's home for dinner, which

I gladly accepted.

Mieka's family consisted of her very nice, intelligent husband, Max, and two adorable little girls, Debora, and Annie. At the time, Debora was just four years old, and the baby, Annie, only sixteen months. Mieka had a way of making one really feel at home. From that very first time we were together, I not only felt welcome whenever I walked through her door, but a new friendship was born, a friendship that would last all through the War.

It was not long after that memorable first visit that I received a phone call from Mieka, imploring me to "come over right away." As I hung up, I knew something terrible had happened. I got there as fast as I could. When I arrived, she was in tears. Max had been arrested. Someone had given him an extra Ration Card and he sold it to his bookkeeper. The bookkeeper was caught cashing in the extra rations and, under torture by the Gestapo, confessed that he bought the card from his employer, Max. Now Max was in jail. All we could do was hope that he would come back somehow. But, once arrested by the Nazis, it was like being in the grip of a ferocious animal that would not release its victim.

Weeks went by without a sign of a trial, and our pessimism grew. The house was rather large, and Mieka was understandably afraid to stay there all alone, so she begged me to come and live with her for the time being, returning "board and a nice home," as she put it, for my kindness and the much needed moral support. I told my parents I would stay with Mieka for a while. Though very concerned, and worried about my moving in with Mieka, they half-heartedly consented.

Max's best friend, Karel, who was then the chief of the Department of Labor in Amsterdam, as well as one of the key members of the Dutch Underground in Amsterdam (unbeknown to the Germans), told us about the terrible plans the Nazis had for the Jews — we would be deported to concentration camps in Poland, and once there, we would be put to death. It first started as a rumor, but soon there was documented evidence, and suddenly everyone knew about the deportations and the murders. Now, Jews by the thousands went into hiding like trapped animals, unable to find a way to escape. As fast as the horrifying news spread, hundreds of good people just as quickly formed organizations to help us. Those organizations became the branches of the Dutch Underground.

My father was released from the Dutch army on a German order as an officer non grata – not wanted because he was Jewish. In an effort to protect his family, he contacted some people he knew he could trust. One of the worst things in those days was the fact that no one could be trusted, and everyone's integrity was in doubt. People turned Fascist because of need and hunger, hoping their new connections with the N.S.B. would give them and their children more food to eat and clothes to wear. An empty stomach was often behind decisions one would never otherwise consider. In a few days, my dad managed to find a place for me to go — a hideout. But this move turned out to be impossible due to circumstances preventing my departure.

APPROACHING DANGER

Our performances, even those in the Jewish theatres, had come to a halt. German headquarters had ruled that "Jews do not need any entertainment" and thereby ordered a stop to all performances. They took over the theatres, using them as temporary confinement for the thousands of Jews they were deporting to the death camps. My people were herded into the theatres like cattle, and treated as much less than that. And by this time, the Nazis had fenced in the Jewish section of Amsterdam with barbed wire, which was not far from our home, converting it into a "ghetto."

There shall no evil befall thee, neither shall any plague come near thy dwelling.
Psalm 91:10

One day, on my way home from Mieka's house to visit my family, I heard people screaming and saw them running, disappearing in all directions. They ran like hunted animals. The German Schutzstaffel (S.S.) were running them down. Not understanding exactly what was happening, and not knowing what to do, my first thought was to run also. I spun around, and just as I started to run, a tall policeman blocked my way. Looking up, I thought I was hallucinating. There, with a big grin on his face, stood my former boyfriend, Kees, in full storm trooper regalia. These storm troopers were full-fledged Dutch "policemen-turned-Fascist," who had joined forces with the German S.S. This dreaded group of turncoats was being used to assist the S.S. on "matters concerning the Jews." The S.S. knew full well that, for the most part, the Dutch policemen who had patrolled the Jewish section for years would not cooperate with them, so they secured the cooperation of the storm troopers. Kees advised me, with the sweetest of smiles, to go home as quickly as possible. The storm troopers were going to route the Jewish people off the streets, grab as many of us as they could, and deport us to Poland to our final place of execution.

Kees then offered to take me home, as it was "safer" to have a police escort. I dared not refuse, and since I was not far from my parents' home, I consented. On the way, Kees asked if I was still living at home. Searching for some glimmer of good in Kees, I was dumb enough to tell him the truth — that I was not living at home but was staying with my friend, Mieka. Then, masking his real intentions, as I found out later, Kees asked me for Mieka's phone number so he could "warn me" each time he knew of German raids. This way, I could be prepared and hide. Naively trusting him, I gave him Mieka's number. He smiled and wrote it down, and as I thanked him for his "kindness," I entered my parents' home, wondering if I would ever see him again. After all, I had spent five years of my youth with him, and really thought he loved me. I never even remotely thought that giving him Mieka's number would cause terrible trouble for us in the future.

It was not long afterwards that a former friend of Kees told me that Kees was now a Gestapo agent persecuting the Jews. I was shocked by this for two reasons. First of all, in spite of all Kees' faults, I thought I still had feelings for him. Secondly, and far more importantly, I now had reason to fear him. I realized that Kees, knowing that I was not staying at home, which was required by German law, could become my most dreaded enemy since he was now a Gestapo agent in possession of Mieka's telephone number.

A few weeks passed. Then one afternoon, when Mieka and I were at home, her phone rang. I happened to pick it up. On the other end a man's voice said, "How are you, my dear?" I knew it was Kees. My first impulse was to slam down the phone. As thoughts raced through my mind, it struck me that if I hung up now, Kees would be furious. That would only pave the way for his revenge, which would be very easy, now that he belonged to the Gestapo. Like lightning, I decided that, come what may, I would speak with him.

After a few minutes, Kees told me he could hear my radio very clearly, and asked if I knew that we were not allowed to listen to the English broadcasts. The Nazis and their collaborators hated those anti-Nazi programs almost as much as they hated us Jews. I told him we were listening to a Dutch program, but that I could clearly hear his radio playing in English, and I wondered how he was allowed to listen. He told me they were not only allowed, but at times required to listen to the broadcasts. Menacingly, Kees told me that he could very easily report me. He asked if I was aware of that fact. I was terrified, but jokingly tried to convince him that he would never do such a thing to his former girlfriend.

Unfortunately, this was like giving him an invitation. He dropped the subject altogether, but wanted to know when and where we could meet for a date. Thank God I remembered that Kees had told me he was now married. Clinging to this last straw, I answered that now that he was married, I could not possibly date him. I knew very well that even if I ignored this fact and agreed to meet with him, that would surely give him an opportunity to trap me with one thing or another. Kees continued to try to convince me that he "loved" me, but using his marriage as an excuse, I kept refusing.

Then there was silence . . . Suddenly, his voice became very nasty and harsh, and he snapped: "Don't worry, I'll meet you, somehow, somewhere," and he slammed the receiver down. By this time, I was shaking badly. Putting the phone back in its cradle, I sank into a chair unable to think lucidly. Hearing his voice in my head, it seemed to spell out the word — "disaster!"

I never forgot those sinister words as the future rolled along: "I'll meet you somehow, somewhere." After the war, I learned that Kees, assisted by Gestapo agents and the storm police, personally commandeered the raid of my cousin's home. The Gestapo dragged my cousin's family outside, and then took them to Gestapo headquarters. From there, they were deported to Poland. The entire family was wiped out. Kees knew my niece, Rose, personally. She was a fine young pianist, who at times accompanied me at my concerts. My guess is that Kees hoped I would find out and panic, and thus give in to his pursuit. But I did not.

Naturally, his revenge didn't stop there. In the following years, Kees' words haunted me wherever I went. I was constantly afraid that one day he would catch up with me, and I was always on guard. If I had only known that our Dutch Underground did away with him long before the war was over, I would have been spared much anxiety and many moments of, as it seemed, almost insurmountable fear. It wasn't until three months after the war was over that I learned Kees had been killed by the Dutch Underground, who considered him to be very dangerous, indeed. I was almost surprised that I had no emotion at all left in me, as far as Kees was concerned. The only thing I felt was satisfaction, that one of my people's and one of my personal greatest enemies had been dealt with as he deserved. Kees met with a traitor's end. I was only disheartened that he had not been caught earlier, before he accomplished so much of his ghastly business.

BEDLAM AT THE THEATRE

By now it was 1942, and the Jewish theatres were shut down. Nazi raids were enacted very systematically. Gestapo agents, together with German storm troopers, slowly drove their patrol cars armed with machine guns and rifled soldiers through the streets, while the S.S. dragged Dutch Jewish citizens out of their homes. These citizens were then housed in the Jewish theatres to await deportation to the death camps.

The Jewish Council appealed to the artists who had previously performed to please help the pitiful people now held captive in those theatres by the Nazis. Thus, when the Jewish Council approached us, Mieka and I became social workers of a sort. We began one of the most heart-wrenching acts of mercy I know of, namely, trying to comfort the many hysterical parents and their children, all doomed to die.

The only thing Mieka and I could really do was try to console them. We gave them some food, which was so kindly provided by the Jewish restaurant manager, Mr. Buschnach. Alas, I did not know how to pray then, or how to give them spiritual food. We saw many dear ones there for the last time. The cries of those to be deported, the children screaming, the sick and the aged, all filled with fear of the unknown. It is impossible to describe, and it was more than we could bear. Our hearts ached continually as we went about our tasks. Old, young, teenagers, children, toddlers, babies, ill or healthy, it didn't matter — all were earmarked for death and no one could escape.

My Uncle Joe was eighty-seven years old. They took him and his

The Dutch Performance Theatre, now popular war monument in Amsterdam, was where Frieda and Mieka volunteered to help the Jews of Amsterdam. Here, the Jews were hoarded by the Nazi razzias before being transported in cattlewagons to death camps.

dear wife, my Aunt Rosie. On the other hand, my very young cousins were deported, as were all the members of my immediate family. Only my brother Bernard missed deportation. Those who were deported were killed.

The turmoil surrounding the lack of hygiene in the theatre was indescribable. Only two washrooms accommodated 9,000 people, and there were only 800 to 1,000 theatre seats. No wonder that lice and disease ran rampant almost immediately. Ever since Holland was occupied by the Nazis, we were denied normal hygienic products, such as soap, which caused lice and vermin to multiply in plague-like proportions.

A curfew was imposed upon us. As no "Jew" was to be seen on the streets after 8:00 p.m., Mieka and I could not go home to sleep. So we slept in the theatre, usually on a bare mattress or on the floor. Any coverings, such as blankets, were totally out of the question. The Nazis routed an average of 9,000 people a day through the theatre, which gave us plenty to do. By the time we finally did go to sleep, we were so exhausted that even an old, dirty mattress seemed inviting.

DEBORA GOES INTO HIDING

As mentioned earlier, my dad found a place for me to hide. But now, working in "the theatre of doom," I was one of the unfortunate ones to catch both lice and scabies. As it would have been unforgivable, unthinkable even, to infect someone else's home with this contagious twosome, I had to refuse the offer of a clean, safe hiding place. We decided that Debora, Mieka's oldest child, would take my place. When the man from the Underground came to Mieka's house to take me to that shelter, we told him the truth about my condition and asked if there was any possibility of hiding Debora instead. He promised to look into it right away.

HENRIETTE AND SIMON

Our next visitor was a lady — and what a lady Henriette was! Her husband, Simon, was one of the finest artists and fancy glassblowers of that time in all of Europe. His masterpieces were displayed in the foremost art galleries in many countries. Henriette and Simon fought the Nazis in a very effective way during that time of danger by using Simon's talents to alter the dreaded Registration Cards. They became two of the truest friends Mieka and I ever had.

Henriette told us she would make sure that the Underground did everything possible to protect Debora, and Henriette herself would become our "contact person." For the sake of the Underground's safety, the people keeping the child, and the child herself, Mieka and I had to comply with the prescribed condition that under no circumstances whatsoever would we try to find out where Debora was, even if it took years. The only thing Henriette would promise was that she would let us know once a month whether Debora was still alive, and if she was in good health.

I do not have to tell you how difficult it was for a mother to have to make that decision. However, there was not much time left, nor was there any other option. So, in desperation, for her child's safety, Mieka decided to give Debora to the organization in the hope that her little life might be spared. Looking out the window, we watched Henriette and little Debora slowly disappear. We saw how the child was crying, and how Henriette had to do her utmost to convince her to come along. Mieka and I both cried our eyes out. I loved that child as if she were my own. Little did we know then that it would take more than three years before we would see her face again.

MAX'S TRIAL

In the meantime, Mieka's husband, Max, finally had his "trial," which was held in The Hague. After he had spent fourteen months in jail, the jury found him guilty of selling a Ration Card. He was later deported. Needless to say, you can guess who made up the jury. Mieka had been informed of the hearing and attended the trial. She told me that not a word of Dutch could be heard, except from the Dutch wardens who took Max away. We never knew to which camp Max was transported. After the war, Mieka was told by the Red Cross Information Service that her husband had been sent to Riga in Latvia, and that he presumably had died there.

ANNIE IS "ADOPTED"

With Debora somewhere in Holland, Mieka and I were still faced with the problem of Annie's safety. But Karel, with the Department of Labor, came up with a brilliant solution. He had papers forged stating that Annie was his child, and in this way he and his wife, Truus, became Annie's adoptive parents. And so, shortly after Mieka parted with Debora, she had to say farewell to her baby, Annie.

The child went to live with Truus and Karel, and would not know for years to come that "Auntie Katrien," who came to visit her once in a while, was really her mommy. Strangely enough, as if she sensed it, Annie would scream hysterically and cry as though her little heart was breaking each time Mieka left. What anguish for a mother not to know where her eldest child was, and to hear the youngest one call her "Auntie," while addressing others, even though they were friends, as "Mommy" and "Daddy."

LICE AND SORES

The children were now gone. Mieka and I were left alone in that big house. Mieka was terribly worried about Max's situation and heartbroken over parting with her children. I, in the meantime, was covered with lice and sores from scabies. The sensible thing for me to do was to see a doctor and try to get rid of both. We found a Jewish physician who had been allowed to stay in practice. It took about three weeks to clear up that mess.

Meanwhile, we were still assigned by the Jewish Council to the work in the "theatre of death." We knew, of course, that our turn would come eventually. However, we were told, that because of the work we were doing, we would be one of the very last ones to be deported. I was convinced, somehow, and just knew in my heart, that I would never go. I kept repeating over and over again that they would never get me alive; they would have to kill me first.

No weapon formed against you shall prosper.

Isaiah 54:17

God had other plans for Frieda.

SEPTEMBER 11, 1942:
The Great Escape from Amsterdam

The pressure on the Jews was getting worse, and by now my dad was really worried about Mieka and me being all alone in that big house. One night he asked me what I would do if the S.S. came for us. I didn't want him to worry, so I answered rather flippantly that if they came, I would lock Mieka in the linen closet, and I would hide under the dumbwaiter (a small but very heavy steel elevator used in big homes to send food up from the kitchen and the empty platters back down again, which kept the maid from running up and down the stairs). I said, "I'll take the key with me and then free her after they leave." I also told him this would not happen for quite a while, as thousands of people were to go before us.

There were 80,000 Jews in Amsterdam, and Mieka and I presumed it would be a long time yet before we were required to leave, according to what the Jewish Council had told us. But the very next day, my dad came to Mieka's house to see if, in case of an emergency, what I had been so flippant about could actually be done. He raised the dumbwaiter, and while Mieka and I held the steel cable, he removed some large wooden boards from underneath. Then he asked me to try it out. I stepped into the holding space, approximately one cubic yard, and sat in a hunched position while he slowly lowered the dumbwaiter down on me. It was so heavy, I screamed, "Let me out of here!" telling him "I'd rather go to Poland!" However, I would change my mind much sooner than I could have imagined. After some discussion, we decided to leave the boards out and use the dumbwaiter as an emergency hideout. My dad told us to always have a little suitcase ready in case we had to escape.

About a week went by, and on the night of September 11, 1942, it happened . . . It was our day off from our sad work of looking after the people being held captive in the theatre before their deportation. Mieka and I were quietly relaxing at her home. That night, we listened to some old records and drank imitation tea, as real tea was no longer available. It was an unusually hot fall, and we had all the windows open that night. Mieka had asked me to sing a bit for her, since due to the work in the theatre, there was little occasion to do so. I wholeheartedly complied and sang a few opera arias for her.

Glancing at the clock, we realized it was already 10:00 p.m., so we decided to go to bed and read a bit. Mieka went downstairs to lock the front door, but when she tried to turn the key, it stuck. Taking a closer look, she discovered she had taken the wrong key, so she came upstairs to get the right one. I said, "Mieka, it's late. Just go to bed and forget the door." But she insisted on locking it. The unusual thing about this was that she hardly ever locked that door. Somehow, that night, Mieka was adamant on doing so, and went downstairs again to secure the lock. Now I know that God was leading her to do this, as locking that door became the Nazis' stumbling block.

Like so many other nights, we went to bed and began to read, using a very small light so it wouldn't interfere with the required blackout. In those days, all of Europe was in a blackout, which meant that all our windows had to be covered with black shades. Any light visible from the outside at night was "punishable by law."

Suddenly a car screeched to a halt in front of our house. Within seconds, a tremendous searchlight pierced through even our blackout windowshades. Instantly, I pulled our little light off the wall. We both jumped out of bed and lay flat on the floor so we couldn't be seen. Then we heard them yell: "Yes, here it is!" — they confirmed our address.

This, then, would become our only chance to escape, or if we failed, our death. I began to crawl along the floor towards the dumbwaiter, insisting that Mieka come with me. Meanwhile, making a tremendous racket, the Nazis tried to force open the front door. They smashed the little diamond-shaped window, and would definitely have walked right in if Mieka had not locked the door with that simple Yale lock. Without a key, they were stuck.

Terrified and badly shaken, Mieka and I decided that no matter what, we would never surrender. We immediately crawled under the dumbwaiter, but this time there was no one to let it down gently on us. Where only one week ago I thought I would suffocate all alone by myself, now the two of us were crushed under its weight.

Made of solid steel, the dumbwaiter was unbearably heavy, and the space to hold two people, as I told you before, was only about one cubic yard.

Actual dumbwaiter seen in the background of this photo, taken before the war.

It seemed as if we were under that dumbwaiter for hours. The noise downstairs increased by the minute. The Nazis were trying to break in through the front door using axes, but were unsuccessful. Suddenly the noise abated and an eerie silence followed. Apparently, they went to our next-door neighbors, very lovely people with whom we were rather friendly. Their daughter, Katja, studied voice with me. We heard them speaking very loudly, demanding that our neighbors tell them if they knew Frieda van Hessen. Now we knew they had come for me! This was Kees' response to my refusal to date him. How else would they have known my name?

The Nazis then asked if I still lived next door. They answered that no one had seen a soul in that house for weeks. We found out later that those good people really presumed we had left. Then, without asking their permission, the Nazis, assisted by the Fascist Dutch storm police, they told us later, entered their house. After searching it, they went into their yard and climbed over their fence into our yard.

By this time, people were gathering on their back porches to see what all the commotion was all about so late at night. The Dutch police called out, asking if anyone had seen people in our house lately. Most of them didn't answer, and those who did denied having seen anyone, except for one man — the milkman! (In those days, milk was still delivered to the house.) He was known to be a Fascist. He yelled back that he had heard me singing that very night, and that he was sure we were there. That was all the Nazis needed to hear.

It was as if the gates of hell had opened! Armed with rifles and the tools for breaking in, the S.S. stormed the back doors of our house. The doors were made of steel, with wired glass on top. Using much force and making a lot of noise, they broke the glass but weren't able to get through the doors after all. They took our neighbors' ladder and climbed to the roof of the garage, which, during normal times, we used as a sun deck. It also provided an entrance into the house through two giant glass doors.

The tremendous noise made by the large glass panels shattering made us realize that they had smashed the doors entirely and were able to get inside.

Now, looking back, I understand what the Scripture means by:

A thousand shall fall at thy side, and ten thousand at thy right side, but it shall not come nigh thee.

Psalm 91:7

Once inside, the S.S. were confronted with yet another door leading to the hallway. That door had been locked by the "Verwalter" — the German official who was given charge over Max's business after Max was arrested. It was locked to prevent Mieka, or anyone else, from continuing Max's electrical parts business. And so, for the time being, what the Nazis had done in the name of evil by putting this Verwalter in charge, worked out in our favor. Unable to open that door, the Nazis seemed to have lost their zeal, and we heard them say they would go to the Verwalter to get the keys. I guess by that time they really thought no one was home!

It is impossible to describe our agony — not only while all that was going on, but after the Nazis left. First of all, Mieka and I were not only paralyzed by fear, but literally with pain. The raid lasted approximately forty minutes. After it was over, however, a terrible uncertainty settled upon us. Had they left a guard downstairs in front of the house? If that were so, he would surely hear the slightest noise and we would be shot the minute we tried to escape.

After listening for a long, long time, and not hearing anything that would betray a guard, we decided to risk it. We were almost certain we wouldn't make it, yet we had to try. After having come so far, we didn't have much choice. With a combined effort, Mieka and I inched the dumbwaiter high enough to get Mieka out from under it. We had been squashed in such a small space for such a long time that our bodies were partially numb. My legs felt absolutely lifeless, folded as they were, not only under the pressure of my own weight, but that of the dumbwaiter.

Both of us were black and blue from the dumbwaiter initially coming down hard upon us. And though Mieka's legs were all right, her shoulders, and in particular her upper left arm, looked horrible. The entire top of her body was black and blue. With her own body in agony, Mieka pulled me out as best she could, and after helping me to the bed, she tried to massage my legs with her one good arm to get the blood circulating again. It was then that we discovered that all that time, the window *next to the dumbwaiter* was open a couple of inches. The Nazis did not see it — all they had to do was to open it and grab us! God had protected us!

If we were to escape, I would have to be able to walk, or there would not be an escape at all. After a while, life returned to my legs. I tried to stand up, but now it felt like millions of needles had been injected into my flesh, from my hips all the way down to the very tips of my toes. After some exercise, but still with what seemed like thousands of needles left, I managed to get dressed. Mieka, trying to get into her clothes, suddenly discovered that she could not raise her arms. I managed to get over to her, and after helping her into her dress, we prepared for our escape.

When the war broke out, Max gave Mieka a batch of diamonds that she could sell in case of an emergency. They had hidden the diamonds very carefully behind a panel of the stairwell that led to the attic. The first thing we needed to do, of course, was to open up that panel and get the diamonds out. Mieka and I also had two fake Registration Cards which we had bought from the Underground.

Those cards belonged to non-Jewish people who gave them to the Underground to help the Jews. The Underground had put our photos on the cards, but the signatures and fingerprints were those of the other people. Mieka and I had trained ourselves to duplicate the signatures perfectly. And so that night we each lost our own identities and became Gentiles.

Upon my father's advice, we had a little suitcase packed and ready for several weeks, with a few pieces of clothing in it, just in case. Such foresight! The narrow stairs to the attic and the roof had been padlocked by the Verwalter, so we forced the lock open with a pair of pliers in order to escape. Armed with the diamonds, the Registration Cards, and the little suitcase, we climbed the staircase to the attic. By the time we got there, it was 5:30 a.m. We opened a narrow window, and began the difficult job of wriggling ourselves through the opening. We decided that I would go first. Once I was outside, it would be easy for me to pull Mieka through. So as not to betray ourselves, we had turned our light-colored trench coats inside out, allowing the moss green lining to show instead.

I managed to get through the window, and I stood, or rather balanced myself, on the very edge of the gutter on the roof, five stories above ground, and leaned against the shingles. Our plan was that I would try to wake up our neighbors. But now came the dangerous part. In order to get their attention, I'd have to knock on their window. We figured there was only one way to do that: I would throw myself over the gap between the two buildings and try to span the distance. Mieka had two daughters who needed a mother, as their father's life was in Nazi hands. Therefore, we decided that I would take the risk. We embraced, as I could easily drop to my death between the two houses. Then, while Mieka held on to my ankles, I plunged forward. I barely made it! I rapped with my ring on the window.

My neighbor, Katja, had a brother who was a sailor with the Merchant Marines, and he was very seldom home. Whenever he was home, though, he slept in the attic. Now I realize God had planned it all ahead of time — he was home! If he had been at sea, we could have knocked until doomsday and no one would have heard us. But, thank God he was home. As soon as he heard us, he jumped out of bed. Yelling for us to hold on, he ran downstairs to get help. Within seconds, the whole family was upstairs, and together they succeeded in pulling us in through their window. Everyone was weeping. They kissed and hugged us. Their tears were freely flowing — for pity, and compassion, and joy. They told us that they had really believed we were not home, calling us heroes for defying the Nazis the way we did.

Now we had to prepare for the second part of our escape. We had to undo ourselves from the hated yellow stars with the word "JEW" in the middle, which were sewn onto our clothes. This was done quickly. After a tearful goodbye, and "God be with you," we wandered into the streets, instantly becoming "the wandering Jews." The strange thing, however, was that now without our stars, we were even more terrified. We were not only afraid of being recognized, we were really scared to death.

Four years later, it was confirmed that the raid on Mieka's house was, indeed, planned and executed by my then-Gestapo, ex-boyfriend Kees. It was probably his revenge for my refusing to go out with him when he called me that fateful afternoon.

THE BEGINNING OF ANNIHILATION:
Danger on All Sides

MR. BUSCHNACH

Mr. Buschnach, the manager of the restaurant at the Jewish theatre where Mieka and I were assigned to help with the deportations, had told us that in case of an emergency, we should get in touch with him immediately. He would then give us an address to a clandestine location in Holland where we could hide. Thus, our next move was to contact him as soon as possible.

We arranged to meet with him, and he gave us the address: 16 Molenkrocht Place in Tilburg, in the province of North Brabant, in the southern part of Holland. Of course, we told him how grateful we were, and that when we arrived at our destination we would let him know if all was well.

But there was another problem I had to take care of: My forged Registration Card said my profession was that of a housemaid, and I did not particularly look like a maid. I would have to undergo a drastic makover.

"FARM GIRL"

Among my pupils was a tenor whom I knew to be a professional hairdresser. I called him and asked him to meet me at a friend's house. When he arrived, I asked him what wonders he could do with my appearance so no one would recognize me. He took a good look at me, and with a straight face told me to get rid of my hair — at least most of it. I reluctantly agreed and said, "Go ahead."

He cut my beautiful, long, dark brown curls until there was almost nothing left. It was a very short "Dutch boy" cut, which looked positively horrible on me. And then, to make things worse, he told me he was going to bleach what little hair I had left. He went to work with peroxide and managed to bleach my poor hair very quickly, turning it into a yellowy straw color. When I looked in the mirror, I was horrified! I didn't even recognize myself — I looked like a carrot. But I had to give him credit. Now I definitely looked the part; I looked exactly like a farm girl who had just come to town.

THE FAMILY ESCAPES

The next morning at 6:00 a.m., while it was still dark, Mieka and I left for Amsterdam's Central Station. We were terrified of being recognized, so we left as soon as the general curfew for our area was lifted. We took the train to our new destination, and to our completely unknown future. This was the first link in the chain of many tragic events to come, but, unbeknown to us, God was always our guiding light.

Before Mieka and I left, my mother came to say goodbye. We cried bitterly, uncertain if we would ever see each other again. My dad could not face this, and he was also fearful that after failing to capture me at Mieka's, the Germans would look for me at their home. That put him and my mother in danger. However, our God, whom I did not know at that time, must have been supporting me in my decision because nothing could stop me from leaving with Mieka.

As it turned out, my idea was, indeed, correct. I was a professional singer, and well-known. My picture regularly appeared in the weekly radio magazines. That was one of the reasons I changed my appearance. But even with the drastic change, staying at home in Amsterdam would have been sheer suicide. Now on the train, Mieka and I were really terrified! Every passenger could be a Fascist, as far as we were concerned.

We figured it would be a little easier once we were outside Amsterdam, and we presumed it was less dangerous for us in Tilburg. I had never performed in that particular area, in the south of our country. Finally, when the train started to move, we relaxed a bit. However, in order to go to Tilburg, we had to transfer at Hilversum, the town where the big radio broadcasting studios are, and from where I had broadcast many, many concerts.

While awaiting our transfer at Hilversum station, I recognized a group of artists on the platform. Imagine the fear of being spotted by them! One of my colleagues, who had been on the stage with me, saw me and came over, saying, "Hello, Frieda! How are you?" I told him that he must be mistaken, that I was not the right party, to which he quipped, "Don't be silly. I know that you are Frieda. You don't have to be afraid. I am okay." He meant that I could trust him. But, Mieka and I were so afraid of betrayal that I just kept denying it.

Our train arrived just then, and Mieka and I got on as fast as we could. I felt terrible for having to deny that sweet man his kindness, and much more so later, when I was told that shortly after our meeting on that train station platform, he had suddenly died of a heart attack at a very young age.

It seemed our trip went on forever, until we finally arrived in Tilburg. Before we left Amsterdam, our friend Mr. Buschnach told us we would need a password to get into the house where we were to stay. We rang the bell, and when the door opened we said the required "magic word," allowing us to enter our first place of hiding. We were immediately welcomed by the Gentile owner and were shown upstairs to our room. There we put down our "belongings," which consisted of our one and only little suitcase. Then we were introduced to the other Jewish "guests" — eight of them in all. They were hiding out also.

MOM AND DAD ESCAPE

The first few days were quiet, nothing special happened. However, one thing that kept bothering me was the thought of Kees' "revenge" that my dad had talked about before I left. Finally I ventured to ask our host if he would go to Amsterdam for me to check on my parents. I told this man exactly what happened, and wondered whether he would also be willing to put my parents up for a few days until the Underground could find them a more permanent place. He very graciously agreed, and the next morning he went off to Amsterdam, taking a letter from me to my parents, in which I begged them to return with this gentleman to the place where I was hiding.

Apparently, our host and my letter convinced my parents that they were in life-threatening danger, and when he returned, they were with him! Mom and Dad stayed only a few days, and then were ushered by someone from the Underground to the town of Bussum. During their trip to Bussum, my parents were told that the Nazis had, indeed, been to their home on the very day after they had left. The Nazis had attempted to fetch them instead of me! They had escaped just in time! Finding no one there, the S.S. viciously took revenge by chasing the poor Jewish people living one floor below us, the van der Ham family, into the street, throwing them into paddy wagons and deporting them to concentration camps. After the war, our Gentile neighbors told us about this vengeful act, and how the storm troopers had taken not only the whole van der Ham family, but also their elderly boarders, who were staying with them during their advancing years.

UNCLE RIKO

My dad's brother, Riko, refused to go with the S.S. when they arrived at his office to deport him. Three times they ordered him to go with them, but he kept refusing. Uncle Riko had absolutely no intention of cooperating, so they shot him, killing him instantly. As his son, Bob, was going up the stairs to the office, he was met by the S.S. They told him that his father had "just died like a hero," apparently acknowledging Uncle Riko's courage. When Bob went into his father's office, he saw my uncle slumped dead over his desk. For some unknown reason, the S.S. did not apprehend Bob, who went immediately into hiding.

EDDIE AND MARIE ESCAPE

My youngest brother, Eddie, and his wife, Marie, both escaped for the time being, working on a commercial liner going up and down the Rhine River. Marie later told us that the captain, knowing all about their predicament, but being an extremely rough and mean person, used them only for heavy labor in exchange for a place to sleep and hardly any food to eat.

BERNARD AND DAISY

My older brother, Bernard, and his wife, Daisy, although they were also in hiding, became very active in Underground work. One of their many achievements was saving several American pilots who had been shot down over our country, and were, fortunately, picked up by the Underground. Before getting the pilots safely out of the country, Bernard and Daisy even kept them in their own hideout, which was a tremendous risk to take. For their action, they received a presidential letter of gratitude, and a medal from the U.S. government.

Since Mom and Dad had left our home too, the whole family was now dispersed. There would be times in the future when no one knew where anyone else was.

ESCAPE FROM TILBURG

Several weeks after we arrived in Tilburg, I overheard the following conversation:

> **Mr. D.:** How nice of you to come and visit us here. But how did you hear about our address? How did you find us?
>
> **Mr. X.:** Well, I knew from Buschnach that you were in Tilburg, so when I got here, I asked a milkman who was parked in front of the station if he knew of a house where Jewish people were hiding out from the Germans, and he gave me this address . . .

For heaven's sake! My heart almost stopped from the shock. I ran upstairs to tell Mieka what I had just heard and insisted that we get out immediately! "Imagine!" I said, "If the milkman in front of the station knows, the Germans will know too! We've got to get out of here right away!"

I called our friend, Mr. Buschnach, the restaurant manager, and begged him to meet with us right away. He came the next day, and we were able to convince him that although we knew hiding out from the Nazis was precarious, the way they did things in this town was a hazard to our very lives. Thank God he agreed and promised to go to The Hague, to a singer I knew there, to ask her if she would put us up for a few days. But when he arrived there, he was told that the family had just moved to Amsterdam.

Quite desperate about our situation and not quite sure how to get us out of Tilburg, Mr. Buschnach had an idea. He bought a newspaper, looked through the ads for furnished rooms, and decided to look at the room advertised on Daniel Street. When he asked the lady there about the room, she told him he had come too late. The vacancy was already filled, as she had just rented the room out to someone the day before. "But," she said, "Why don't you try the other side of the street? That is a rooming house, too, and maybe she still has something available."

Thanking her for her kindness, Mr. Buschnach left for the other side of the street. The woman there indeed had a lovely place available. While they were discussing the price and conditions, he happened to mention his talk with the lady across the street. "Oh, boy," our new landlady said, "it's a good thing you didn't rent from her. I'm sure your friends wouldn't have liked it there — she's a Fascist and belongs to the N.S.B.!"

God had protected us again.

ESCAPE FROM
DANIEL STREET

Our room was on the second floor. It was a beautiful room, big and airy, with a little enclosed porch attached. Mr. Buschnach had told our new landlady that he was renting for two ladyfriends of his who were now in the south of the country, but were coming to live in The Hague the next day. No explanation, nothing. He paid our rent in advance and called us in Tilburg, telling us the address. We packed our little suitcase, told our host we were leaving, said our goodbyes, and set out for our new destination — our SECOND hideout.

Our new landlady was very kind to us. For the first time since we escaped from Amsterdam, we were less frightened. We even began to feel "at home."

It must have been about ten days later that Mr. Buschnach paid us an unexpected visit. Just by looking at him, we knew something terrible had happened. His eyes were red from crying, and when we asked him what happened, he began to sob. He told us that the house where we had been staying in Tilburg had been raided by the Nazis, and everyone, including our lovely Gentile hosts, was deported to Poland on an S.S. "punishment transport." Those punishment transports were even worse than the regular transports; all of the people were handcuffed to prevent escape. Among those captured in that house were Buschnach's best friend and business associate, the man's wife, and their little daughter. He heard from bystanders that when the child screamed and tried to run away, the Nazis shot her, killing her right in front of her parents. They almost lost their minds when that happened. And not one of those poor people ever came back.

Terribly shocked, we wept with him. What an incredible place the world was becoming. Human beings were turning into vicious animals, killing left and right, uprooting everything that was once beautiful and peaceful. But those poor people . . . What had they done that was so terrible that they should suffer so?

Our friend, Mr. Buschnach, left. Whatever became of him, we will never know. Some people told us he escaped to England and got married. Others said they heard he was deported and killed. We never saw him, nor heard from him again. I am afraid he died also. If he were alive, I am sure that somehow he would have tried to contact us, like others did after the war.

THE HEROIC LANDLADY

Life returned to "normal" again, that is, for us it went back to the point where we could sit and wait for the next event. Then, one day, our landlady came upstairs and asked for our Ration Cards. She was supposed to receive a certain number of them for each room she rented. The decent thing to do now was to tell her the truth. So, with some trepidation we told her we were Jewish. She was very, very kind about it and said we could stay as long as it did not get her into trouble.

It was a German regulation that Jewish people married to non-Jews, whether male or female, were not to be deported until the end of the war. On the third floor of our rooming house lived such a couple. Several weeks went by without any disturbances — no more than the ordinary trials of watching and waiting, of false alarms and whisperings. It had become second nature for us to whisper for fear that others would overhear and betray us.

Totally unexpectedly, one night at 3:00 in the morning, our landlady ran into our room. She was still in her nightgown. Ashen-white, she whispered to us the words we feared more than any others: "Get out! Get out fast! They're upstairs!" We jumped out of bed, and while Mieka dressed in a flash, I literally threw the folding bed together and up against the wall, as if no one had been sleeping there. We had agreed to do this when we told our landlady that we were Jewish. If anyone ever came for inspection, she was to tell them these were her living quarters.

According to German law, all boarders had to be registered, but when we told her we were Jewish, naturally she could not and did not register us. Now at 3:00 in the morning, the Nazis insisted on inspecting the house. They started with the first floor and went according to the list of boarders.

The instinct of self-preservation makes people sometimes say or do things which, under normal circumstances, they would never have thought of. So, in this case, when the Nazis started on their round of inspections, our landlady blurted out that the husband of the couple on the third floor was Jewish. She knew that these so-called "mixed marriages" were safe, but realized that mentioning the word "Jewish" might distract them, and in so doing she might be able to divert their plans from inspecting the second floor to the third floor instead. It worked, at least temporarily. After she led the Nazis to the third floor, she excused herself, stating that she wanted to put on her housecoat. Then this sixty-five-year-old-lady ran as fast as she could to our room to warn us to get out before it was too late.

Everything went incredibly fast. Mieka was dressed in a minute, but by the time I had the bed ready, there was no more time for me to put on my clothes. I slipped into an old skirt, threw my trench coat over it, and stepped into the only pair of shoes I owned. With the curlers still in my awful looking, straw-blond hair, without proper underwear, no top, no stockings, we ran into the street, into the pouring rain. We kept running as if the devil himself was after us, until we reached the house of Harry, Max's schooldays bosom buddy, who now happened to live in The Hague with his Gentile wife. We hoped he had not been deported. The incredible miracle of this escape was that we were running in a totally blacked-out city, and though Mieka had been at Harry's only a few times, we found the address.

We rang their bell and kept on ringing until the door opened. Harry and his wife were terribly shocked, and terrified that it was the S.S. coming to grab Harry. Every Jewish person lived literally day and night with this devastating fear. They took us in right away and helped us get out of our soaking wet clothes. While we told them what had happened, they gave us some hot soup, hot tea, and some dry clothes to rid us of our chill. We stayed for the rest of the night and tried to sleep a little, which was not easy.

The next day, Harry's son went back to Daniel Street to find out from our landlady what the raid was all about and if it was safe for us to return. Extremely frightened after this experience, our landlady told the boy that we could come back only to gather our things, but she did not want to be "part of the game" any more. She also told him that the woman across the street, where Mr. Buschnach originally wanted to rent a room for us, belonged to the N.S.B. and had something to do with the raid. She had earlier made the remark that "those two ladies staying at her rooming house seemed to be in an awful hurry last night . . . " Even at three in the morning, she apparently did not miss a trick! When "coincidences" like that occurred, we knew we were victims of a traitor, and our landlady knew too. We went and packed our few things, and tried to contact the Underground to find out what our chances were of finding another place. Meanwhile, we decided to stay at a hotel for a few days. We looked in the advertising section of the daily paper and chose from several ads.

FLIGHT FROM THE HOTEL AT THE HAGUE

When we entered the hotel, the receptionist asked for our Registration Cards. She carefully copied our names and numbers onto a specially designed form which, we found out later, would be checked within 24 hours by the Dutch police. This was apparently another new regulation, unknownst to us who were devoid of newspapers and radio broadcasts. We were certainly not aware of its peril. Each police precinct was now in possession of the so-called "black book," which carried the names and numbers of all Registration Cards that were "lost or stolen."

Of course, by this time the Germans were well aware that at least ninety percent of those cards were neither lost nor stolen, but plainly given to the Underground so they could in turn be given to help save Jewish lives. Those working for the Underground forces not only changed the photos, but were able to change the fingerprints as well. So far, Mieka and I only had our pictures on the cards, as it was quite expensive to alter the fingerprints.

When Henriette had come to Amsterdam to take Debora, Mieka's oldest daughter, she also gave us her home address, to be used only in case of an emergency. She also lived in The Hague, where our hotel was located. At this point, Mieka and I were truly desperate for a new hideout. We decided that this certainly was an emergency, and that our only recourse was to contact Henriette and Simon. We called them, and Henriette told us to come over to their house, which was an artist's studio, right away. There we met Simon, her husband, who at that time was, as I mentioned before, one of Europe's most outstanding painters and fancy glassblowers, and whose masterpieces were displayed in most of Europe's Fine Art Galleries. Not only was Simon a great artist, but he was a great humanitarian. Both of them were so good to us, and had such high ideals of justice, and especially of freedom for all — every race and creed. We will always remember them, with love, with great admiration, and above all, with great respect.

The minute we were inside their home, they asked if we had registered at the hotel. When we told them "yes," they panicked. "You've got to get out of there! they replied. "You can't even go back to get your suitcase! Don't you know that your Registration Cards are being checked right now in the "black book?"

That's how we first heard about the "black book." We almost had heart failure — we were absolutely terrified. Henriette decided to take the matter into her own hands. She would go to the hotel and tell them that "those two ladies who registered the night before" were her personal friends, and that she had invited us to stay with her for the rest of our vacation. Henriette was taking a terrible risk. If the Gestapo had found out that we were Jewish, they would already be in our room and would have her arrested.

Once in the hotel, Henriette rushed upstairs, packed our things, raced down again, paid the bill, and got out of there as fast as her legs could carry her. Outside, she met Mieka, who was waiting on a quiet side street to help her carry the suitcase. Meanwhile, Simon had asked me to stay with him to go through the "black book," a copy of which the Underground had given him to be used for his work in altering Registration Cards. Checking whether our numbers had been entered, after a while we indeed found them, in black and white, right in the book! Mieka and I had again made it through the eye of a needle. Truly, our God was protecting us!

Because of his artistic ability, Simon altered the numbers on our cards so beautifully that no one — not even a professional — could have detected it. His talent was being used especially for this purpose by the Underground, and only God knows how many lives were saved because of his efforts.

KLAUS

Shortly thereafter, we contacted my brother, Bernard, who was a very active Underground worker himself while hiding. Being Jewish made this doubly dangerous for him! Bernard had a German friend, Klaus Gentz, who was the son of the director of one of Germany's foremost universities. He was terribly anti-Nazi, as were his parents. The Nazis had forced his father to sign party membership, but when it came to Klaus, they were unable to coerce him. In refusing to cooperate, Klaus placed himself in grave danger, and the only way out, therefore, was to escape from Germany. But how? The poor man walked for days and finally reached the Dutch border.

There he met a man who happened to own a brewery located near the border. Risking that this man might himself be a collaborator, Klaus told him of his dilemma and asked if he knew of a way to get through the border unnoticed. The brewer had what we call "a stroke of genius" and suggested that Klaus go over in a beer barrel, which would be rolled across the border into Holland, just like any other beer barrel was rolled every day of the year except

Sundays. The Dutch plant in Holland received the barrels, which were then prepared for delivery throughout the country.

Accepting this offer in good faith, taking the man at his word, and thanking him for his help and for his marvelous suggestion, Klaus crawled into a beer barrel. They made two air holes for him and closed the barrel on both ends. Then he was rolled off a slide, and Klaus was on his way to freedom. He rolled into Holland and into the open arms of the Dutch Underground, who had been notified by the beer manufacturer of Klaus' unusual arrival!

The Underground welcomed Klaus as their own as soon as he contacted them. Although they were constantly on guard for traitors, after checking Klaus' story and finding it to be entirely true, the Underground was all too glad to have such a fanatical anti-Nazi on their side! Both Klaus and his wife, Ursula, were instrumental in the Underground's resistance to the plague of Nazism that was rapidly spreading across Europe.

GEERTJE: *A Collaborator after All*

My brother, Bernard, who had gotten to know Klaus through the Underground, asked him to find a hiding place for us. Klaus succeeded. He then came to our temporary shelter at Simon and Henriette's house and took us to a certain woman in Bussum named Geertje. She owned her own home and was willing to put us up. We accepted the offer, however, the price was very high, both financially and personally.

Bussum became the town where Mieka and I would spend approximately two years in two rooms, hiding from the Germans. Geertje was a divorcee who lived with her very old and very nasty mother, and her six-year-old daughter. Once we had settled in, we discovered that Geertje had innumerable "boyfriends," most of them German soldiers. Because of this situation, we spent most of our time in bed to avoid making any noise, as she spent much of her free time in her bedroom, which was next to ours, in rendezvous with her different lovers.

Meanwhile, Geertje was shrewd enough to tell us that in case the Germans should lose the war, which to her was absolutely out of the question, Mieka and I would have to demonstrate how "generous" she had been towards us. We would have to stand on the balcony with our Stars of David sewn back onto our clothes, yelling "we are Jews" to the neighbors. The neighbors appeared to be quite disgusted with Geertje, turning their heads whenever they met her, as they were aware of her affairs with the Germans. She planned to convince them after the war that her affairs were only covering the fact that she was hiding Jews. But everyone knew the truth. Geertje never fooled anyone.

The Canadian forces later quartered in Bussum, and not aware of her former Nazi connections, also patronized her services. The only difference was the fact that they spoke English instead of German. Everyone knew, and certainly we did, that she only kept Jews in her house for financial gain. She charged us an arm and a leg, and I thank God for Max's foresight in providing the diamonds! Geertje did not help out of compassion, as many others did, some even sacrificing their lives. How different her attitude was from say that of Henriette and Simon! They never asked us for anything, and they even went so far as to refuse the financial assistance we offered for the many risks they took. They went through innumerable perils to help hundreds of people in the same manner. They put a high value on human life and fought for their principles.

While we were hiding out in Bussum, I realized that the shock of our initial escape in Amsterdam, in September 1941, had affected my memory. Although I could clearly remember all that had happened to us, I could not for the life of me recall the simplest piece of music. As time went by, slowly, oh so slowly, parts of melodies suddenly penetrated that dark part of my mind. With great difficulty, I was able to recall and to patch pieces of music and words together. One time, while struggling to recover my memory, I started to sing out loud. As soon as the old woman, Geertje's mother, heard me sing, instead of politely asking me to stop, as it would be dangerous if others heard me, she sent the little girl upstairs with the following message: "That Jew upstairs must shut up, or we will tell the Germans on her."

Of course, these were the old woman's true feelings of hatred and anti-Semitism. There are no words to describe the hurt and the bitterness in our hearts. We were fighting for our existence, and now we knew that the very people we were depending on despised us. If they betrayed us, it would mean certain death.

Another thing we had to put up with were the fleas. We'll never know where they all came from, but Geertje's house was infested with them. I remember killing ten of them in one night. There is positively nothing that racks the nerves more than not being able to sleep properly because of a continual itch. They bit me as if their lives depended on my blood. Our complaints to Klaus about our hosts' bad attitude and the fleas were to no avail, as there was no other place to be had. We had to stay. Life was dangerous. It had become a macabre dance between death and freedom.

By this time, my parents, who had also escaped from Tilburg, had apparently met with new trouble in their hideout and had contacted Klaus via Bernard's Underground connection. Klaus asked Geertje if she knew of someone who would take them in. She mentioned the name of Mrs. de Weerd, the lady who lived next door to her. She told Klaus that the woman was anti-Nazi and needed money badly, so there was a good chance she would take in my parents. She promised Klaus that she would suggest it to her, and then would let him know. Of course, Geertje must have told Mrs. de Weerd the price that she was demanding for our stay. She contacted Klaus the next day and told him that Mrs. de Weerd was willing, but only for the same high price that she herself was charging. Klaus told my parents of the financial condition and they accepted.

In a way, we were reunited. Although it was very dangerous to visit them, at least we knew they were close by. Some nights, Mieka and I would steal through the bushes and slip unnoticed into the front door of Mrs. de Weerd's house. My dad had made an emergency hideaway in the attic, with the approval of Mrs. de Weerd, and installed a short wave radio there to hear the latest war news from England. He listened every day to the English broadcasts to keep up with the progress the Allies were making towards winning this terrible war. He was anticipating a normal life again for the Jewish people, should we survive.

It was like living in the days and times of Moses. We were being trampled by the enemy and, as in those days, we were praying for and awaiting our liberation. It was the same old story, only in a different setting. Then, it was the "civilized" Egyptians and their Pharaohs who tortured us, killed us, and starved us to death in Goshen. Now, it was the "civilized" Germans displaying the high standard of their civilization by killing us in concentration camps. This was the "enlightenment" of the 20th Century — "kill all the Jews . . . "

During those days in Holland, there were only two topics of conversation, even among the most intellectual people — "the war" and all the misery that went with it, and "food." Today, living in the wonderfully free country called America, where, thank God, no one is forced into doing things they do not want to do, and which is truly a "land of milk and honey" for those who are willing to put in an honest day's work, it seems almost paranoid for a person's thoughts to revolve around food all the time. During the war, however, it became an obsession. Only if people in the free world would be forced into starvation, as our occupied country was, would they be able to understand this compulsion and constant focus on food. My obsession was for RAISINBREAD! I stilled that craving plentifully after the war!!!

At one time, Holland was one of the richest countries in the world — a land of plenty. Then, suddenly, we were put on a severe diet, which in reality was nothing but starvation of the Dutch population. We could hardly exist on the amount of food allotted to us. Now and then, Mieka would sell one of the diamonds Max had left her, and with the money she first paid for our hideout quarters in advance, and then used the remainder to buy some food, which was priced extremely high in the stores because of the black market.

The black market was thriving. People were paying thirty dollars for a loaf of imitation bread made of a tiny amount of wheat mixed with ground-up flower bulbs, twenty-four dollars for a bar of imitation soap, one hundred twenty eight dollars for a pound of meat, if it was available. These excessive amounts were charged in the years 1941 to 1945. No bargaining was possible; either you paid for it or you didn't get it.

Mieka divided the good and expensive food among us, my parents, and my mother's niece, Esther. Mieka was very good to them, indeed. I had saved as much money as I could while I was performing, but by this time there was nothing left, and my parents' money was slowly ebbing away. To have no money was like having an axe held over our heads — no money, no hideout. The worst of it all was that no one knew how much longer this war situation was going to last. Money then meant life itself.

The progress of the Allies, no matter how fantastic and fascinating, seemed hardly enough to make our one dream come true — the dream of liberation, of redemption from the yoke put upon us by the occupying forces, being a free people again. Freedom for all, Jew and Gentile, as many untold numbers of Gentiles were suffering too. Yet victory and freedom still seemed a long, long way off.

Being forced to stay in only two rooms made the days feel endless. During that time, I knitted the same red sweater eight different ways. For lack of wool, as soon as it was finished I would unravel it and begin another one. To keep myself occupied, I tried each time to knit a different pattern. I also read Dostoyevsky's *Crime and Punishment* aloud to Mieka three times, as well as *The Idiot* and *Gone with the Wind*. Mieka, because of stress and anxiety about her children and Max, had a nervous condition in her head and neck, jerking it to one side. She was therefore unable to read, so I read interesting books to her.

PANIC AT THE MOVIES

One night Geertje came home and told us that the next evening she intended to have a cocktail party for her German friends. I know this sounds completely unbelievable, but along with this announcement, we were informed that it would be too dangerous for her to have Jews in the house at that time, so we were told to spend the night elsewhere! This would not have been so bad if we could have gone next door to my parents. But, when we suggested this, it turned out that both landladies had already agreed that it would be too risky for both of them to have Jews in their homes when the Nazis were present. Therefore, my parents' landlady told my parents that they could not receive us, and that she preferred if they went out also.

We decided it would be impossible to roam the streets all night, as that was risking arrest by the German police, so we decided to go to the movies. We went to one of Bussum's movie theatres and were watching a Czechoslovakian picture when, unexpectedly, a woman's voice said loudly enough for us to hear, "I bet you they are Jews . . . I bet you all the money in the world they ARE JEWS." Whether or not she had noticed our uneasiness or self-conscious attitude I cannot say, but suddenly the man got up. We all froze.

What should we do? Running would give us away completely, and they would run after us as fast as they could. We all just sat, totally petrified. I remember my heart skipping beats from sheer fright.

A couple of minutes later, the man returned with the theatre owner, who flashed a big light on us. There was commotion among the other theatregoers, and my heart was beating as though I were facing a firing squad. The owner told my dad and Mieka to get up and come with him to his office. We, who were left behind, were having the most fearful thoughts of what was going on there in the back of that theatre. My mother, Esther, and I were positive that we would be taken next. Already I had visions of how we would all be deported to Poland the very next day.

At last they returned. My dad's face was ashen and he did not speak at all. Neither did Mieka. Now we were watching the movie, seeing nothing, hearing nothing, only hoping that it would be over soon, so we could get out without making it too obvious. Walking out in the middle of the movie would have made it look like an escape. Finally, after what seemed like hours, the show was over and we left the theatre. As we got up from our seats, we heard the woman behind us say to her husband that she was convinced that we were Jews, and "if she were the boss, she would have us all arrested and killed, like the rest of those Jews!"

Once we were outside, we didn't dare look back, fearing that we were being followed. We walked slowly in the direction of our hiding place as if nothing had happened, although we would have liked to run as fast as our feet could carry us. We were scared to death; we were hunted animals in human form.

When we were a safe distance from the theatre, we checked to see if we were being followed. Seeing no one, Dad finally started to talk. He and Mieka had been taken to the office to face "the law." Thank God there was a Dutch police officer on duty that night. He gave them a long look, and then asked for their Registration Cards. Glancing at the cards, he said, "I don't see anything wrong with them." And then, turning to Mieka and stroking her raven-black hair, he said, "I love black hair." It was his way of letting her know that he knew she was Jewish but would not arrest them.

As I mentioned before, most of the Dutch policemen were not only loyal to their country, but they really liked the Jews. This man had, just for appearance's sake, copied Mieka's and Dad's names and addresses from the Registration Cards, and then told them to go.

When we got home, the "party" was over and our landlady was already in bed. We had been told not to come back before 11:00 p.m. Everything around us seemed peaceful, but we were far from being at peace. We were terrified that perhaps the officer's address book would be checked and our names found in it. Staying fully dressed, not even covering ourselves with a blanket, we were ready to run at the first hint of danger. Mieka and I just lay atop the bed, unable to sleep a wink, fearing that a paddy wagon could pull up at any moment and soldiers would drag us out of the house. Four days and nights we endured that agony. Then, trusting that the officer had indeed been a loyalist, we dared to relax again.

Just as we had hoped to get some rest, someone came to visit. His message both excited and horrified us tremendously. He was a trusted liaison sent by Henriette and Simon. Disaster had come to those two lovely people. They had been arrested. Someone had betrayed them, and they were caught in the act of retouching Registration Cards. The Gestapo found an envelope with our return address in Henriette's pocketbook. Henriette grabbed it from the man's hand and tore it to pieces, hoping he would forget the address. He slapped her across the face and arrested her along with Simon. The Nazis threw them in jail.

Dear Henriette had been racking her brains to find someone she could trust to warn us not to contact them any more. She found out that this man was going to be released and, hoping that he would not be a collaborator, she relayed her message to him. As the story was told to us by that gentleman, we realized that she feared the Gestapo might come for us. But all along, God was looking after us. Of this, I am now absolutely certain.

So that same night, in the darkness, we visited Klaus, who also lived in Bussum. He took us in and allowed us to stay only for a few more days, as he could not have us there for any length of time. He had to be vigilant because of the Underground work he was doing. It would not have been safe for us there anyway, since he himself, like Henriette and Simon, was constantly in danger of being caught and arrested. In a different way, those patriots' lives were in as much danger as ours, if not more.

The Germans always worked very quickly, so we figured that if they had not been to the house within three days, the coast was clear and we could go back. We surely did not mention any of the happenings at the movie theatre to Geertje, who would have put us out in the street the very minute she knew. We only told her that we were going away for a few days. After three days, we asked Klaus to phone her. He asked her if he could speak to us, and she answered that we were out of town for a few days. By her answer, we knew that the coast was clear, or else she would have reacted differently. The danger was past, at least for the time being. So we returned in the dark and the still of the night.

After the war, Henriette told us that Simon had been a real hero. He had argued with the Nazis back and forth, insisting that Henriette was absolutely innocent, completely unaware of his Underground activities. Finally, they freed her, but Simon was deported to the horror camp of Dachau, where he was killed. May this wonderful human being rest in peace. Henriette, God bless her, though all alone now, was like a piece of granite. She kept up the fight for freedom all through the war.

TRAGEDY STRIKES EDDIE

Bernard and Daisy were living somewhere in a basement apartment in Utrecht. As far as we knew, Eddie was somewhere in Brabant on a farm. At least that's what Bernard had told us. Later, only after my continuous anxiety over my kid brother, Bernard finally decided to tell me the truth. Eddie had been betrayed. He had a connection — a lawyer — who was supposed to supply him with proper papers so he could work and earn some money for his upkeep. In truth, this man was a double agent. He was officially working for the Dutch Underground but, unbeknownst to them at the time, he was also engaged by the Gestapo. Through him they found out all they wanted to know about people receiving clandestine Registration Cards. When the date was set, Eddie was to meet a certain person, who would then hand him his papers. Instead, Eddie found two Gestapo agents in civilian clothing waiting for him. They grabbed him and took him to Gestapo headquarters, and from there he was deported to one of the most gruesome concentration camps in Poland — Auschwitz. Bernard begged me not to say anything about it to Mom and Dad until the war was over. But as it turned out, they would never know.

Eddie played the violin beautifully, and it was the one thing he loved more than anything else. No matter where he went or what the circumstances may have been, his precious violin always went with him. And so, this time also, when he was arrested and deported to Poland, the only thing he had with him was his violin. After the war, I happened to meet a Jewish doctor who had survived the same camp. He remembered Eddie well, and at my request gave me some details about what he went through. He told me that while the Jewish people were herded into the so-called showers, which in reality were the gas chambers where they were killed, Eddie had been forced to play his violin. I believe it was the mercy of God that cut short his life. He contracted typhoid and dysentery and lay dying for several weeks because the doctor was not allowed to look after him properly. The doctor told me how he had loved Eddie, and how courageous my little brother had been all the while. Because of the shortage of medicine, the doctor said it was impossible to save his life. I believe that as Eddie was dying physically, he also died from a broken heart, being the sweet, sensitive, little brother that he was.

MARIE

Meanwhile, Marie, Eddie's wife, was also deported to the same concentration camp. Marie and Eddie never knew of each other's presence there.

Marie miraculously escaped death. After the war, she told us how, in the women's camp, all those poor victims of the Nazi barbarian sadists were forced to walk daily in a gigantic circle, barefoot, sometimes through the snow, with hardly any clothes on their starving, weakened bodies. A "kapo," or overseer, was placed at the exit of the camp. The kapo's job was to give just a light tap on the back of the persons of her choice. The "tapped" people had to go to the exit, from where they would start on their "journey of death" to the gas chambers. The scenes that Marie spoke of, especially of the younger people, the teenagers who were afraid to die, begging on their knees for their lives, screaming for help which could not be found, the utter despair of it all, defies description. Just like the tick-tock of a clock, the lives of these women were being tapped away. Marie escaped this cruel tapping five times. Each time, it was either the person in front of or behind her who was chosen.

Then, one day, Marie was mistakenly put on a transport to Theresienstadt in Czechoslovakia. Those transports were usually made up of intellectuals who were being used to promote ideas toward the one goal the Germans had in mind — namely, to rule the world. Because of this mistake, Marie's life was spared.

Once in Theresienstadt, the Nazis took her more than 100 feet under the earth, where for nine months she worked in an underground airplane factory, starving on the most unheard-of rations of water, one slice of bread, and one potato a day, and being beaten so fiercely that her body is still covered with large scars. For those nine months, Marie and the others never saw daylight.

Eventually, when the Russian troops arrived, she was liberated. However, her misery had not come to an end yet. The Russians tried to rape her and the other women in the compound. Marie fled to the mountains, weighing a mere eighty pounds. She dragged herself along, dressed only in the remains of what had once been a blouse and skirt, until she passed out.

When she finally regained consciousness, Marie found herself lying in a large bed on a farm owned by a Slovakian farmer and his wife, who had found her more dead than alive. They could not converse because of language differences, but the good farmer and his wife understood, and tried to make up for all the suffering the poor girl had gone through. They fed her, clothed her, and were like a father and mother to her. They kept her on the farm until she had gained thirty pounds. Only then did they allow her to leave to go back to Holland. They had made certain, via the Red Cross, that some of her relatives had survived the war.

But the biggest shock awaited Marie. When she returned, she heard for the first time that Eddie had been in the same camp and had lost his life there. The heartbreak, the tears, the indescribable sadness she must have felt, for she had loved him so much.

Marie also remembered a promise she had made. While she was waiting to be deported to a concentration camp in Westerbork, Holland, there had been a lady with two small children who were, like Mieka's children, placed in different homes with different families to find shelter from the Nazis. Emaciated and exhausted from all the stress and misery, this little lady died in Marie's arms. Before she died, she pleaded with Marie, as her dying request, to promise that if Marie ever returned from that hell, she would try to locate her children and her husband. She asked Marie to look after them if they were still alive.

And so Marie started her inquiries about them with the Red Cross. She asked them to find out if they were still alive, and where those children and their father might be. The Red Cross found that they indeed were alive, gathered all the information for her, and arranged for the father and the children to meet Marie. At this meeting, Marie told him that his wife had died in her arms, and that her last request was that Marie, if she survived, should look after her children and husband "as if they were her own."

Though this man sadly missed his wife, and Marie was heartbroken losing Eddie, they came to an agreement. They both decided, for the children's sake, to marry as soon as possible and to provide these youngsters with a home again. They were determined to try to make something good out of their own broken lives. But, no matter how much people try, we cannot force love.

They did marry, and Marie looked after the children for years as though they were hers. She was also blessed in having a child of her own. Liesbeth, out of this union, became the joy of her life. But, in spite of it all, Marie could not forget Eddie, and though she had hoped to find happiness with this new husband, it was not meant to be. When the children were of an age that they could look after themselves, Marie separated from a very unfaithful husband.

THE BLACK LIMOUSINE

Geertje had acquired a new habit of visiting us, uninvited, to have tea in our room almost every afternoon. Mieka would chat with her more than I did, and I presume Geertje thought she was rather welcome. Believe me, nothing could be further from the truth, but of course, we could not very well refuse these visits under the circumstances.

During one of those "teas," Geertje confided to us that her Nazi captain boyfriend had offered her twenty-five guilders for each Jew she would betray and for each illegally possessed radio set. You can't imagine how we felt. It was as if ice water ran down my spine, and I could hardly breathe for shock. However, Geertje kept smiling and drank her tea.

It was a little while after she passed this information on to us, in a more or less matter of fact way, that one night, when Mieka was not feeling well, I had a very strong urge to see my parents. There being no moonlight, as it was terribly overcast, I crawled over the ground through the bushes to their hiding place and spent some time with them. I don't know why I felt so compelled to go, as I had never before gone there all by myself. How delighted they were to see me so unexpectedly!! They hugged and kissed me, and little did we know that it would be the last time ever . . .

As we were talking about the war and exchanging different opinions, we got on the subject of "God." I saw that my parents had lost any and all faith that they might have previously had in God. Though they never had talked about God to us children, they rejected the idea that He exists on the basis that if He really did, He would never allow all these innocent people to be slaughtered, Jew and Gentile alike.

Now that I am grown, and I am a believer, I know how God is the axle around which our whole life turns. I am sad to say that Godly matters were never discussed in our home. Therefore, it could never have been my religious instruction that made me argue back. Only my two brothers received religious training. At the age of twelve, they prepared for one year to have their bar mitzvahs, as every Jewish boy at that age does. That is their confirmation, and they are then considered to be men, responsible to God. But that was where my family's religious education ended. And although I had only once been in a synagogue, for the wedding of my brother, my heart told me that God does exist. God had put this truth in my heart, just as Paul explained this spiritual phenomenon to the Greeks in Athens some 2,000 years ago!

My parents laughed at me and told me to grow up. But no matter how they held fast to their opinions, the knowledge of God's existence stayed in my heart, and at that moment I was very much aware that they were fearfully wrong in all that they said and in all they thought regarding God.

I tried to convince my parents, telling them that I knew in my heart that somehow God would, in His own time and in His own way, reckon with those who were hurting us and killing us now. I emphasized that all their doubts would not do them any good; that God had given us all an equal chance to choose good or evil. He surely would take revenge, if it were indeed true that the Jewish people are His chosen ones. How did I know all this? I later recognized that the Holy Spirit was speaking through me.

That was the first time in my life I felt so positive about God. However, I did not know "the Word of God" as the gentleman in black back in Germany had called the book he had given me. I had been too scared to read it, and now, alas, I lacked the knowledge to convince them.

After we said our goodbyes and kissed each other once more, I crawled back to the house, back to Mieka, back to the unreal life we were leading. This time I had a great sadness in my heart, like a foreboding of some calamity about to strike us.

The next morning I faced the greatest tragedy of my life. It was very early when we heard a car stop in front of the house. In our minds, any car spelled danger. We knew that a car, in those days, was associated with the Nazis. Instantly I knew that destiny was calling at our door. I jumped out of bed and peeked through the curtains, and saw a long, black limousine parked in front of my parents' hiding place. It was surrounded by civilians curious as to what was going on, and by several German soldiers armed with rifles and machine guns. The Nazis were ready to shoot anyone trying to escape, as if three poor, weakened people could have harmed them.

Mieka and I were petrified, just standing there as if nailed to the ground, waiting. But we did not have to wait long. We saw them come out. Poor Dad and Mom with ashen-white faces were followed by my mother's niece, Esther. All three were surrounded by soldiers with bayoneted rifles. My sweet parents never looked up to where we lived for one second. They just kept on walking towards that car. They knew that even one glance up to our windows might betray us too. Then they entered the limousine that whisked them away, out of sight forever, away from those who loved them so dearly.

ESCAPE FROM BUSSUM

I reacted like a bomb exploding. I began screaming and crying, almost hysterical with grief, and no one could stop me. My tears ran like a wild river. I was wild with the rebellion that was boiling over inside of me. Then, like a figure of doom, Geertje stood in the doorway. Pointing her finger at us, she told us to get out — immediately! That was just about the only thing that could have brought me back to my senses and stop my fit of despair. The need for self-preservation became a reality that overrode my other emotions, all my feelings of heartbreak, shock, and rebellion.

Mieka and I threw what little clothing we had into our one small suitcase, which had already served us for several escapes. And so we fled again. But where were we to go? There was no place, and certainly not in daylight. And then, I remembered "the letter." The very thought of it overwhelmed me. "The letter! The letter!" I stammered. I had written a letter to my brother, Bernard, which I had left the previous night on the table in my parents' room. They were to give the letter to Mrs. de Weerd, who would mail it the next morning at the post office. And now I realized, as the raid had been around 7:00 a.m. that my dad never had time to hand the letter to Mrs. de Weerd! Consequently, the enemy was now in possession of my brother's address.

We were frantic. We raced to Bernard and Daisy's in Utrecht as fast as we could to tell them to escape before it was too late. We were sure the Gestapo would come after them.

THE AFTERMATH: *Panic at Bernard's*

The minute they saw us, they knew something was wrong. Our sudden appearance, our faces so pale and tear-stained told the story. But Bernard and Daisy thought it concerned Mieka and me. They assumed we had been thrown out. When we told them that our mother and father were gone, Bernard let out just one scream, then cried and cried. We all did.

I told them about our letter to them and its fate, and that it most likely had come into the wrong hands. Then, just like us, they packed their things and we all ran. We presumed, and much later were convinced, that Geertje had a hand in this terrible drama. We remembered the unasked-for information about the twenty-five guilders offered for each Jew she would betray. We wondered how anyone could stoop so low as to sell a human life for any amount of money. But then, Judas did the same thing, betraying our Lord for thirty pieces of silver.

After the war, when Geertje had to appear before the courts that were trying and imprisoning collaborators, she insisted that she had confided to the druggist that her neighbor was hiding Jews. She maintained that she had not betrayed them. However, the druggist denied it all, and no one was ever punished as there were no witnesses . . .

Bernard immediately contacted the Underground. Mieka and I were separated for the first time. Up until this time, we had been together, and were somehow relying on each other's strength and moral support. Now, however, I was totally alone in the house of a lady I had never seen before. She was an Underground worker associated with Klaus. I was staying in an attic room with no one to talk to all day long, day after day. I became more and more despondent. I never was so miserable and lonely in all my life. After a few weeks, I begged my brother to find a place where Mieka and I could be together.

UTRECHT AND AMSTERDAM

Without warning, my new landlady had to get rid of me for some Underground reason, and just like a package, I was transported to another address. This time it was a big, beautiful home in the city of Utrecht. This was the hideout of Daisy's brother, Dick. I was to be kept there for a few days only, until the Underground could find a place for both Mieka and me.

After nine days, I was told that Mieka and I would be taken to Amsterdam. For me, this was the most dangerous place in the world because of being well-known from concerts and performances! We were going to live in the house of a Mr. Spykstra, an old man who lived alone, only one block away from Mieka's former home. No sooner had we arrived than we were informed by the Underground connection that the house in Utrecht we just escaped from had been raided by the S.S. Everyone there, including Daisy's brother, Dick, had been deported to Poland. It was truly like a dance macabre, but on each occasion God had Mieka and me dance away just in time.

We also learned that the S.S. had indeed gone to Bernard and Daisy's hideout in Utrecht to do away with them . . . Our warning about the letter had come just in time. Later, Bernard heard from Klaus that my dad had confided to a Dutch police officer at the precinct where they were being held, and whom he thought he could trust. He was concerned about the letter, and had begged the man to contact Klaus so he could also warn Bernard.

The Dutch police officer told Klaus the following story. My mom and dad had to hand over their Registration Cards. The Dutch inspector looked the cards over carefully and handed them back to them. He said he saw nothing wrong with them, and told them that they could go. However, there was another inspector present, a known Fascist, who wanted to check their fingerprints.

You may recall that obtaining a card with one's own fingerprints involved quite a lot of money — 300 guilders for each person. Since my parents' finances were getting low, they decided to wait a while. Maybe it would all be over soon. They kept postponing it because the English-speaking radio stations continuously were broadcasting news of the coming invasion by the Allies. My parents had hoped to stretch their finances so they would have enough for the hiding place and food until that great day of liberation . . . If only they had paid for the real fingerprints, it might have turned out differently. When the Dutch Fascist inspector found out that the fingerprints on my parents' Registration Cards were not their own, Mom, Dad, and Esther were doomed. They were thrown into jail, then eventually deported to Poland, where they were killed in the gas chambers of Auschwitz.

We learned after the war that Mom and Dad had found out about our Eddie being in Auschwitz. Witnesses told us that upon hearing this news, my parents suddenly became two old, broken people who gave up the last bit of fight left in them. They knew what was waiting for them — we all did. They even left the personal possessions they had with them behind in Westerbork before being transported to Auschwitz. I am told that the only thing my dad said was, "We won't have any need of this where we are going. Keep it." Little did he know, however, that one item in particular, a "whist" card box, would fall into the hands of Eddie's wife, Marie. She recognized the box that belonged to my parents, which they used when they played "whist," a card game, with Uncle Ali and Aunt Stella, who were also both killed at Auschwitz. It was in that way Marie found out her in-laws had been deported, while she herself was awaiting deportation to Poland from camp Westerbork.

And here we were, Mieka and I back in Amsterdam. Another hiding place, another host, and more of the ever-present possibility of unexpected trouble awaiting us.

THE OLD DRUNK

Old man Spykstra was divorced and had a girlfriend, and both of them were drinkers. After a little while, he started making advances towards Mieka, who would have no part of him. This didn't stop him from trying, of course, and all day long he tried to convince her that she should get rid of me. This was all to no avail, as Mieka and I had gone through too much together. Neither one of us would leave the other. That was understood, not unless circumstances forced us to do otherwise.

As time went on, old man Spykstra realized the futility of his pursuit, and he began to drink all the more. The dangerous part was that when he drank, he talked too much. We were terrified that he would tell his drinking buddies about us. And he demanded a very high rent. It saddened us to see all of Mieka's good money being wasted on alcohol, with the possibility of losing our very lives to boot.

It was also understood that because I was well-known, I should not go outside at any time. But Mieka, who with her raven black hair looked more Indonesian than Jewish, was allowed to go shopping, and went a few times a week to the neighborhood grocer.

THE CHARWOMAN

It was on just such an occasion, when Mieka returned from an errand one day, that she happened to look back through the little window in the door and noticed a woman jotting something down on a piece of paper. When the woman looked up, Mieka recognized her with great shock — it was her former cleaning woman.

When she came upstairs, she told me about it. I asked her only one question: "Did she like the Jews when she worked for you?" "Definitely not," Mieka answered, "in fact, she's blaming all of us for the disaster of her daughter's marriage to a Jewish man." Consequently, I had only one reply, "We've got to get out of here as soon as possible!"

Mieka began to cry. Extremely depressed from all the running we had done so far, and terrified of the future, she refused to go. I told her, "You can stay here if you want to, but I'm leaving." She begged me to stay, but my mind was made up. I just knew in my heart we had go, and quickly, before it was too late.

FORCED TO ESCAPE . . . AGAIN

I had the same premonition as when we left Amsterdam that very first time, when we escaped over the roof, and in Tilburg, where even the milkman knew about Jewish people in hiding. I felt this time just like I felt then, that I was doing the only sensible thing I could. In my mind, there was no choice. Finally, when Mieka saw that I meant business, she packed her things. Leaving a note and some money for Mr. Spykstra, we left. Once again, we were out on the streets. This time we were in the heart of Amsterdam, where I was born, raised, and now, much to my disadvantage, very well known.

How can I describe the fear with which we walked those streets? My heart was pounding like a machine gun within my chest. We felt as if a giant monster was pursuing us. Was it possible that once we had lived here? That we had been happy here? That we had laughed here? That it was a pleasure to walk those streets that now seemed to threaten us? Was it possible that this once-so-warmhearted town was harboring something evil that was ready to instantly devour the Jewish people?

We went to the office of Arie, who was a business friend of Mieka's husband, Max. We were certain that Arie was an Underground worker and therefore trustworthy. Shocked to see us walking into his place of business in broad daylight, Arie promised to get us a place, and urged us to leave the city at once. But where to? All of a sudden, Mieka had a brilliant idea. She suggested we go to Bilthoven, a beautiful residential place seven miles from the city of Utrecht in the middle of the country, where she and her family used to spend their summer vacations camping in the sandy hills. We left immediately for the train station, miraculously reaching it without being recognized, or running into some unscheduled German raid as I had encountered that time when Kees brought me home.

We took the very first train out of Amsterdam to our new destination. When we arrived at Bilthoven, we went to a hotel where its owner, Mr. King, was a friend of Max and Mieka. He kept for just two days. We phoned Arie the following morning to find out if he had an address for us. We also wanted to find out if anyone had come for us at the address of old man Spykstra. Arie told us to stay put until he arrived that afternoon.

Since he had not answered our coded question, we presumed it had gone badly at Mr. Spykstra's. Indeed, it happened just as I had feared. Mieka's former cleaning woman had betrayed us, and the day after we left, Mr. Spykstra's home was raided by the S.S. They turned everything upside down, and even went to all the neighbors. But, as before, God led us out of this Egypt. Max's friend, Arie, had not yet obtained an address for us, and it was out of the question to go back to Amsterdam, so for the first time we were on our own. And that is how it would be for several years to come, until the war was over.

BILTHOVEN

Bilthoven is surrounded by the most glorious countryside and meadows you have ever seen. Our predicament now was that we had no idea of how to go about finding a safe place to stay without the help of the Underground. Knowing that it would probably be dangerous to stay in a rooming house as we had learned in The Hague, we figured we had to get a new hiding place quickly. We decided to go for a walk in order to think things over, wondering what would be the safest thing for us to do. Actually, we knew nothing was really "safe." We were two homeless women in a war-torn country, and only God could guide us and see us through.

Soon we reached the woods, which seemed like an oasis. It was a haven of peace and beauty. As we strolled along, enjoying the clear, fresh air and the beauty of the forest, we suddenly saw a picturesque little church. When we got closer, we saw that it was a Dutch Reformed Church. Little did we know then that two years later, in this very same church, the most meaningful event in my life would take place. We walked all around it, admiring its Gothic architecture and beautiful landscaping. We wanted to look inside, but we found it closed.

Walking away from this lovely building, we noticed what looked like a rather large, wooden shed not far away. At least that's what we thought it was. But as we drew nearer to the structure, it proved to be a small restaurant. We were starving and decided to go in.

You have to realize, Felicia, that whatever we did, or wherever we went, we were constantly in danger, as betrayal was always right around the corner. But inside the restaurant it was very cozy, clean, and pleasant. A waiter came over to us, and for the first time in a very long while, we ordered an honest-to-goodness decent meal in a restaurant. It turned out to be delicious, indeed.

ENTER JAN BRAUN

While we were sitting there, chatting and waiting for our dinner to be served, a gentleman suddenly approached us and asked if we were comfortable. We smiled at him, acting as much at ease as possible, for he could be a traitor. A conversation ensued, just small talk about everyday life, revealing nothing special on either side — not from him, and certainly not from us! Then, when the meal was served, the gentleman left us alone. We enjoyed our dinner more than any other meal we had had for the longest time, and were finally relaxing over a cup of imitation tea, which was a lot better than the imitation coffee in those days.

The gentleman came back to our table, now asking if we had enjoyed our dinner. Thinking that he was the head waiter, we gave him a nice compliment, highly praising the food and the service. Then he told us that he was the owner. He asked us if he could join us for a cup of tea and he introduced himself as Jan Braun.

As the conversation rolled on, something told me very clearly that we could trust this stranger. And in retrospect, I recognize that what I then called "premonition" was indeed the Holy Spirit guiding this conversation — although in those days, I was absolutely unaware of any guidance in my life. Out of the blue, much to the chagrin of Mieka, who became as white as a sheet, I told him that we were Jewish and badly in need of a place to hide. Then came his most surprising answer.

He said that from the moment he saw us, he presumed that we were Jewish and in trouble, which prompted him to come over to us in the first place. He hoped that, as an Underground worker, he would be able to help us. We were elated! How was it possible that my parents could not believe in God, seeing how He helped us all the time? While we did not even know Him or worship Him in those days, in retrospect I realize how God was watching over us time and again.

Jan Braun said that he knew an elderly couple who might be able to rent us a room. He told us to stay in the restaurant while he went to see this couple, to find out if they would be willing to take us in. When he returned, there was a broad smile on his lovely Dutch face and his blue eyes were sparkling. The minute we saw him, we knew it was all arranged. The couple was willing to rent us a large and airy room. And they were very nice people, indeed.

THE ENGLISH ATTACK

Bilthoven is about fourteen miles away from Soesterberg Military Airport. Airports were the main targets for the Allied forces to bomb in those days, as the destruction of airports and railroads meant fewer supplies for the Germans. Every day we heard the Allied planes overhead, so high in the sky they were almost invisible to the human eye. The sound of the engines thrilled our hearts, knowing that each trip was bringing freedom a little bit closer.

In the city of Utrecht, seven miles from Bilthoven in the opposite direction from the airport, there was a railroad junction. Utrecht itself was like a great arsenal, surrounded by depots filled with ammunition, antiaircraft, and cannons, all of which were needed by the Germans to fight the war. German headquarters for the eastern section of Holland was also near Utrecht. The Allied planes bombed it many times, cutting short German supply lines and killing as many Germans as possible. Unfortunately, sometimes Dutch lives were lost, as innocent people living near those targets could not always escape the surprise attacks.

Once I almost became a victim myself. In a small field behind our hideout house, the Germans had installed an antiaircraft battery. It was in the midst of a populated area, yet quite out of sight. But the Allies were well informed of the Germans' whereabouts and knew of this latest move. I had ventured to go out on a much needed errand, and on my way home, English spitfires attacked Bilthoven without warning. They flew in small formation until they were directly above their target, then they bolted down like lightning, giving it their full measure of machine gun fire, hence their name. Sometimes spitfires attacked trains or military depots, German soldiers' quarters and headquarters, or antiaircraft batteries. The attacks were so sudden that the Nazis had no time to prepare.

The spitfires came down full speed with deafening noise, flying right through the streets. Throwing myself to the ground, I crawled towards a hedge for protection, and just lay there half dead from shock and fear. The attack came as such a surprise to the Nazis that they had no time to fire back at the planes. They could only run for shelter, leaving the antiaircraft battery to the Allies, who completely destroyed it.

Just as fast as the planes had come down, they went up again, straight up into the blue sky, disappearing like something out of a dream. Suddenly I realized a lady was bending over me, lifting me up. With her arms around me, she took me to her house, which was opposite the hedge. She had watched me but could not come out before, as she was too frightened herself of getting hit.

After sitting a while and drinking some nice cold water, I felt much better. When I went outside again, I noticed that the sky had turned to a golden red. I asked a passerby what had happened. He told me that when the spitfires had attacked the antiaircraft, others had come down on the east side of the village and pumped their ammunition into the German headquarters building. It had been a beautiful villa that belonged to some Dutch people before the Nazis had them deported and killed. And now their headquarters was burning to the ground.

There were several casualties among the Nazis. But the most important thing was that by burning their headquarters, valuable papers were also destroyed. Many of those papers would have incriminated Underground workers. Because of this bombing, many a Dutch person was saved from destruction.

Still shaking, I ran home, where I related my experience to Mieka and our landlord. We rejoiced over this attack as though we were celebrating a birthday.

ALLIED ATTACK ON SOESTERBERG AIRPORT

Shortly afterwards came a massive attack on Soesterberg Airport by several hundred Allied war planes. We watched how our beloved "silver birds" flew over, and noticed how they marked their targets with red phosphor lights before the attack. After a few minutes went by, everything started shaking — the house, furniture, dishes, glassware. It all came tumbling down and the windows shattered. Out of sheer fright, we huddled under the stairway, thinking it would be the safest place in the house as there was no basement.

The attack came at noon, on the most delightful, sunny summer day you could imagine. But, within a few minutes, it was like midnight. It was pitch black all around us. The airport was about three minutes' flying time away, and all the smog and dirt thrown into the air when the bombs hit made it impossible to see anything. We later learned that all of Soesterberg's runways had been damaged, and that there were somewhere from 1,500 to 2,000 bomb craters. The Germans repaired this airfield as much as possible, but it would not be long before a massive second attack.

Not only had the airport changed its appearance, but Bilthoven was changed along with it. Bilthoven had become a town with windowless houses. Not a window was left intact — nothing but gaping holes were staring at us. Everywhere, people were putting up wooden boards, since it was impossible to get glass at this stage of the war. The large glass factories in the south of Holland were all closed as railroad supply lines were cut off by the Allies' continuous attacks. We had to get used to the "new look" of once-so-beautiful Bilthoven.

AN UNEXPECTED ENDING

The Germans in Bilthoven were just like little children — scared to death after this attack. But at night, they played the big shot. One night in particular, they put on a real show. Remember, the field had been damaged where they had their antiaircraft, and that was right behind our house. There were also some barracks where the men assigned to this post were staying. That night, maybe to restore their badly shaken confidence, the Nazis decided to raid all the houses bordering the airfield. They came at night, after curfew, to look for "outlaws" as far as their "laws" were concerned. It was around midnight when they came marching through the streets, waking up all the townspeople. The Nazis were always very shrewd in their timing, counting on the least resistance from sleepy people who were not prepared to defend themselves.

Everyone had to open their doors, and in they came, shouting orders to people, telling them to open all their closets, looking behind doors and furniture, into stairways and cellars, to try to find rogues like Mieka and me — people whose only crime was to be born of Jewish parents. We were never really sure of it, but they might have come for us.

Our house was the very last one in the row. We were up in our room in our pajamas, breathless, frightened, shaking all over, panic-stricken, and expecting the worst. But God protected us again. From sheer fright, our landlady had passed out and lay sprawled in the middle of the hallway. When the Nazis came in, they took one look at her and saw that she was not faking — being deadly-white and completely unconscious — and decided to leave, marching right out of the house.

This was all well and good, but what about next time? What would have happened if they had started on our end of the street? Surely we could understand that our landlords had enough from that one scare, and they very kindly asked us to leave as soon as possible.

MRS. DE GRAEFF

What to do now? The next morning, in despair, we turned back to Jan Braun, the restaurant owner, and asked him for advice. Again he spread his antennae to find a safe place for us, and came up with the name of a certain Mrs. de Graeff. She was a Christian of the Episcopalian faith, a wonderful person, who lived with an equally wonderful young son, Bobbie. Just the two of them, they lived in a "miracle home." Jan recommended us highly to her, and it was there that we would stay until the war was over, in spite of the horrendous happenings that would yet occur.

After the war, Mrs. de Graeff told us that although Jan had never mentioned it, she knew right from the beginning that we were Jewish. Jan had only told her that we were hiding from the Nazis because of Underground activities. We moved to Mrs. de Graeff's place, as we had moved into all the other places, hoping that this stop would finally bring us a little rest. But much more excitement was in store for us, excitement of a different sort than we had experienced thus far.

VISITING ANNIE

We were given the large front room, the price was decent, the house quiet, and the people sweet. What more could we want? As time went by, and during the "intermezzos" between persecutions, Mieka's longing for her children became so intense that she became physically ill. Mieka contracted a nervous condition which continuously pulled her head to one side, causing the muscles to stiffen, and resulting in an inflammation of the nerves. It was very painful, and it was really pitiful to look at. But her desire to see Annie was so overwhelming that we finally decided to go to Hilversum, where Karel, of the Labor Department, lived with his wife, Toni, and Annie, their "adopted" child. If you recall, it was impossible to see Debora, as we did not even know where she was. Her whereabouts were a complete and well-guarded secret and were kept from us by Henriette and Simon until after the war.

It was highly undesirable to go to Hilversum by train because of almost continuous spitfire attacks to destroy the railroad tracks. Buses or other public transportation were just not available. The only other way to get there was to walk. Of course, by this time our clothes, and especially our shoes, had worn to such a degree that they not only looked awfully shabby, but it was out of the question to make a seventeen-mile hike wearing them.

I suggested that we at least buy some new footwear. But no matter where we tried, each time we received the same answer: "Shoes? Well, it's been a long time since we've seen them." The only thing we could get a hold of were wooden soles, which could be tied onto our shoes with string. We hadn't worn stockings for at least two years either, and they were nowhere to be found, and not for sale anyway except with textile coupons, which we of course, did not possess. We Jews were labeled "outlaws" and lived on clandestine food Ration Cards supplied to us by the Underground.

Mieka and I decided to buy the wooden soles and, in the bitter cold, with our shabby coats, no stockings, or gloves to warm our hands, we commenced the seventeen-mile hike. To get to Hilversum, we had to cross the "Lage Vuursche" most of the way — a hilly, wooded area stretching for miles. In spite of the cold, our feet burned like fire. We walked until we reached a small restaurant where we could rest our sore limbs for a while, and then go on again until we found, miles further down the road, another place where we could eat something and sit down.

Finally, after many hours, we arrived in Hilversum at the house of Karel and Truus. I remember how Mieka just stood there, tears rolling down her cheeks as she watched her little Annie, now a little girl of almost four years old, for the first time in two-and-a-half years. The nervous tilt to her head made Mieka look even more pitiful. Suddenly, the child asked Truus, "Mommy, who is that lady?" Truus told her that this was her "Auntie Katrien" — Mieka's alleged name. But Annie was a very smart little thing and quipped, "How come I never saw this Auntie before?" Truus told her that this aunt lived very far away and had come from the Indies. Only now, for the first time, she had the opportunity to come and visit her little niece. While winking at Mieka, Truus said that she hoped Auntie Katrien would repeat this visit as often as she could.

The day turned out wonderfully. The reunion, the food so much better than we had grown accustomed to at that time, the kindness, the beautiful home they lived in, all made it a memorable event. We promised Annie that we would come back as soon and as often as possible. But, as if Annie sensed the blood ties that bound her to Mieka, she would not let go of her, clinging to her with all her might, and screaming and crying when we started to leave. She repeated this behavior every time we came to visit. Truus told us that Annie would cry for hours after we were gone, and although she was always very close and affectionate to her "Mommy" (Truus), on those occasions Annie would have no part of her or of Karel. Truus would put her to bed, and only the next day, after a good night's sleep, would Annie be back to normal.

I can't remember, Felicia, exactly how many times we visited Annie or how many times we made this awful, long trek. As often as we did go, never for one moment did we go off the main road to sit down by the wayside. For Mieka and I, who loved nature so much, this was strange, indeed, but we didn't even consider it then. Again, we must have been guided by the hand of God. After the war, the people of The Bilt, Bilthoven, and the surrounding townships were warned by the Allied forces "not to cross the Lage Vuursche" as it was literally covered with land mines planted on both sides of the road. Mieka and I never knew about the mines. We just kept walking on the main path, recuperating only in restaurants. How marvelous are His ways!

THE SECOND BOMBARDMENT

In the midst of so many memories, there are always some that seem to stand out more than others. Sometimes I do not recognize the meaning of these things until later. Often, much later, I realized the purpose and/or influence a certain event might have had upon me.

I remember clearly, for instance, how once in the midst of terrible fear I suddenly became convinced that nothing would harm me. The occasion was an appointment with a gentleman we knew, who was to help us get some dry wood for the furnace. Wood was our only source of heat, as the Nazis had done away with our fuel and coal supply. Wood was also illegal to obtain, and whatever we did get was always wet and needed days of drying in order to burn properly. I was supposed to meet this man at a previously arranged spot in the woods on the other side of town.

It was a bright and sunny but cold and clear fall morning. I had left the house on a borrowed bicycle and pedaled as fast as I could to get warm. The wind was blowing through my hair, and I even felt a little carefree. Just a little though, as one had to constantly be on guard. But I remember how surprised I was to feel that way — almost normal. After all, when one is young, it is very natural to feel exhilarated when the weather is crisp and clear, and one is biking through beautiful countryside.

I must have been traveling about half an hour along my route, and had already entered the outskirts of the woods, when I noticed hundreds of planes circling above. They looked magnificent, like ever-so-many tiny, silver birds, because they were flying at such a tremendous altitude. I remember wondering how those lovely-looking birds could perform such monstrous acts. However, not expecting an attack, but rather thinking they were on their way to Germany, I kept on riding.

Abruptly, a thundering roar jolted me out of my blessed state, and I realized they were attacking right where I was, right then and there. I heard the bombs as they pierced the air with that horrible high-pitched scream.

My first impulse was to lie flat on the ground, as I had done before in the village. But something told me to get out of these woods while I still could. I turned around and pushed the pedals with all my might to gain speed. In a few minutes, I was out of the woods, and I aimed for a house I saw that had an open porch. I threw the bike to the ground and ran. Though I was still in the open, at least I was out of the forest. I made it to the house, the porch being a poor shelter after all. As I stood in front of the door, shaking from head to toe, a great calm suddenly came over me. Someone spoke to me very clearly: "Don't worry, you are not going to be killed. All will be well." I lifted my head, looked up, and said, "Okay, God." Even though I had never been taught about Him, I was convinced of His protection. The door opened and a lady urged me to come in. I smiled at her and confidently told her that I knew that nothing would happen to me, that God had told me so! Confused as to what kind of a person I was, she still tried to convince me to come in because of the flying shrapnel. But something inside me told me that I had to live up to this faith. So I stayed outside, the woman slammed the door in my face, leaving me standing out in the midst of the air attack and the flying shrapnel.

The bombardment lasted from ten to fifteen minutes. The railroads had been blown apart, as well as what was left of our previously attacked Soesterberg Airport and its newly reconstructed runways. We were told the reconstruction cost the Germans a fortune and a great loss of manpower during its restoration.

After the attack, I went to the other side of the street, picked up the bike, and went home. I never met the gentleman who was waiting for me to arrange for the wood supply. Once I arrived at Mrs. de Graeff's house, everyone came running out. Mieka tearfully embraced me, telling me how terribly frightened they had all been, imagining that I had been killed, or was lying somewhere wounded by shrapnel. They did not know exactly where I had gone, and would not have known where to look for me. They were just hoping that I would return "home" safely. I will never to my last day forget the expressions on their faces when I told them that I was not afraid for one second. Reading their thoughts — that I was bragging about my courage — I told them the experience I had of God speaking to me so clearly. Much later, after the war, as I learned more about Him, I realized to an even greater degree that God was protecting me during that bombing.

"VIOLETTA DE VALERIE"

Living in a small town in those days was rather precarious. It seemed almost unavoidable that people would get to know you one way or another. But since every stranger coming to town was looked upon critically, it certainly made it a risky proposition. For fugitives like us Jewish people, it was, of course, very dangerous to mix socially. Yet it was equally dangerous to stay away from people altogether. To tell you the truth, I don't know which was more dangerous. "To mix, or not to mix?" was always the question. But if one decided to "mix," one had to know just with whom and where, as a wrong choice could be perilous.

Mieka and I liked Jan Braun a great deal, and the feeling being mutual, he invited us often to his restaurant where he had a piano. We told him that I was a singer, and he responded that his brother was a classical performer. Having music in common, Jan seemed to enjoy our company. He asked me many times to sing, and supplied sheet music which he borrowed from his brother. Somehow our musical get-togethers became known, although the singing was always done in the morning hours when there were no customers.

Now that many people in Bilthoven knew of my singing ability, it became obvious that I would have to do something about my Registration Card, my second one, which listed my profession as that of a dress designer. I would have to get one with an Italian name to justify my voice and my appearance, as my former straw-colored hair had finally grown out and I had dark hair again. I decided on the name Violetta de Valerie, the name of the role I played in Verdi's *La Traviatta*. Thus, I obtained not only another card and another alias, but both Mieka and I had our own fingerprints put on them as well.

I would have to change my entire background too, just in case somebody might look into it. Mieka and I concocted the following story: I was born in Holland, the child of an Italian father and a Dutch mother. My family had gone back to Italy just before the war but I had stayed to complete my studies at the Conservatoire. The war made it impossible for me to join my parents in Italy. I even wore a beautiful little cross that was given to me, which I hung on a small, silver chain around my neck. Being "Italian," it was likely that I would be Catholic and thereby wear a cross. Somehow, I now felt safer than at any other time since the beginning of the war. I wore that cross day and night.

IMAGES OF THE PAST

Before the War

These images amazingly survived the war thanks to one woman's quick thinking. After the Nazis passed a new law forbidding Gentiles to serve Jews, Maagje, the van Hessen's Gentile servant, was forced to leave the family. Thanks to her kind heart and intuition, she saved what photographs she could, preserving the brighter, happier time before the shadow of the swastika was cast.

Frieda's father, Izak van Hessen, as a young man.

Frieda's mother, Sarlina Diamant, at age 18.

Engagement photo of Frieda's parents.

Van Hessen family photo after Frieda's birth.

Van Hessen family photo with all three small children.

A wonderful day at the beach with grandpa Eli
and the family housekeeper, Maagje.

The van Hessen family and Maagje on vacation in Goslar,
Germany. Bernard at age 11, Frieda at age 6, Eddie at age 5.

Frieda at the age of 14.

Frieda at the age of 18.

Frieda's dad and his
brother, Ali, on vacation.
Both were killed in Auschwitz.

Van Hessen family's first car, the imported "Overland".

Wedding photo of brother
Eddie and Rie.

Frieda's parents' silver wedding aniversary. All but five
present that day were killed during the war.

Frieda's dad was recalled to active duty during the mobilization.
Shown as captain of the Corps of Engineers with two military aids.

Frieda's dad (center) and other captains of
the Corps of Engineers.

The Heartbreak

Frieda, after the war, standing, shocked, in front of what once was her home.

The rectangle outlines a piece of wallpaper left on the supporting wall of what used to be Frieda's room.

The sad and overwhelming discovery was completed when Frieda saw the stones from her home on a flat boat in the Canal.

Mainstreet in the Jewish neighborhood in ruins much like Frieda's home. Homes and stores were ransacked for wood or belongings that were left behind as residents fled or were deported.

After the War

Frieda after the war in this May 1945 photo, clad in her only remaining dress. A life flower is in her hair.

A house belonging to a Nazi collaborator which was later confiscated and alloted to Frieda's family by the government where, for the first time in her life, Frieda read the Bible and found the Messiah.

The front cover of this concert program from after the war features Frieda's last concert tour in Holland.

Translation of program: "Tour, Deen's World Theatre Tours brings Frieda van Hessen, lyric and coloratura opera singer before her departure to America."

Frieda's portrait after arriving in Montreal, Canada. Age 32.

Frieda preparing for an international broadcast on CBC in Montreal, Canada. Age 33.

Frieda at a concert performance in Montreal, Canada. Age 37.

Frieda at a concert at the Richter Estates in Danbury, Conneticut. Age 47.

The van Hessen's housekeeper, Maagje, at age 92.
Photograph taken at the time of Frieda's
speaking tour in Holland in 1996.

Frieda arriving in Greece in 1993 enroute to Israel, visiting the cities and islands of the Agean Sea where Paul preached in the first century.

THE LUMMELS' HOARDING

Among the people we met at Jan Braun's restaurant was a family by the name of Lummel. They were known to be Fascists, and the man was employed as a mechanic at the heavily-damaged Soesterberg Airport. Jan told us to watch out for the Lummels, and believe me, we did. They lived straight across the road from us. Mieka and I figured that if we became friends with them, it would give us an alibi — no one, but no one, would suspect us of being Jewish. Most people knew of the Lummels' connections with the Nazis and were afraid of them. Mieka and I talked it over and decided that the next time we met them at the restaurant, we would get the Lummels to invite us to their home.

Before going to the Lummels' home, we asked Jan to introduce us to the leader of the Underground forces in The Bilt, (of which Bilthoven is part). We wanted to play it safe and let it be known to the right people that we were only mixing with Fascists as a matter of camouflage because of the dangerous position we were in at the moment. We were invited to the Underground leader's home, where we were interrogated by him and three other men. I had to tell them exactly with which regiment my father had been an officer, and what position and rank he held — he was captain of the Corps of Engineers.

Mieka and I were told that if all I had said proved to be true, we would be accepted by the Underground; they would stand by us in case of trouble. Also, we were asked by the Underground to cooperate with them in case they needed us. They might very well have to call on us at some time in the future. We agreed, and proceeded to arrange the date with our "new friends," the Lummels, which automatically started us off on our new career — that of Underground workers.

The Dutch people were really starving. Our rations were decreased to a mere eight hundred calories per day, and everybody, except those who worked for or collaborated with the Nazis, was suffering. The Dutch population's daily food rations consisted of eight hundred grams of bread (mainly crushed flower bulbs mixed with some inferior kind of grain), and ten kilograms of sugar beets (which are normally fed to cows) per person, per week. The cows for the most part, had already been killed anyway and fed to the German army, but the beets kept on growing. What better use could the Nazis put them to than to feed us? In essence, we became the cattle.

Those meager rations were really the Germans' reprisal for Dutch railroad personnel obeying the orders for an "all-out strike," given on behalf of the Allies by our Prince Bernhard in London. This strike handicapped the Nazis to such an extent that, instead of going to the frontiers, German relief troops had to drive Dutch trains in an attempt to have some form of transport for their supplies. The Germans warned us that they would kill the strikers, starve our entire population to death, and that we would all be jailed. But their threats were to no avail. The strike continued, and it was one of the most effective strategic blows dealt to the German war machine by the Allies, via our Dutch government in exile.

Meanwhile, many, many people, probably thousands in Holland were dying from hunger. It eventually became "normal" to see long processions of folks with their old carts and worn-out baby carriages lining the highways, walking to the farms to sell whatever they possessed, like linens or jewelry, in exchange for food. The farmers were shrewd, and many of them took scandalous advantage of their own starving countrymen while they themselves still had plenty of food hoarded away. The very strain of pushing the cart for miles after obtaining the so desperately-needed food was too great for many a man or woman, and often they would drop dead on the road. To make matters worse, the Nazis frequently would confiscate the hard-earned, precious goods from people while they were on the road, leaving them materially destitute, emotionally devastated, and humiliated. Physically pressed as well, many then snapped into a rage, which caused the Nazis to arrest them. In the cities, adults and children were dying from malnutrition. Parents unable to save their children's lives were devastated with grief. This time was later called "The Hunger Winter of 1945."

Mieka and I borrowed an old baby carriage from a neighbor, for which we had to give them potatoes in return, and filled it with twigs and wood gathered from the forest. We then took the carriage all the way to Utrecht, where we gave the wood to Bernard and Daisy, who had found a new hideout but were freezing. They did not have the advantage of living near a forest like we did. Bernard knew a farmer and exchanged my jewelry and fine woolen camisoles for dry goods like peas and beans, which we took back in the baby carriage. For this we walked eight to twelve miles to Utrecht and back on what we called "shoes," however they were merely wooden-soled sandals. This was a horrible winter, but, after all, we had to eat.

The Lummel family, meanwhile, had enough food stored away to feed a whole army. Mr. Lummel had grown rather attached to us, as we were the only people willing to associate with them. He appreciated that we were nice to his children, and he even became very informative about their way of life and their activities. Once, after drinking a good deal of gin, Mr. Lummel began to brag about all the good things the Germans had given him. He showed us the two fabulous leather overcoats they had just been given that very day. He then told us that he had enough food stored away in his attic to last him and his family through the end of the war, and insisted on Mieka and me going upstairs to the attic so he could show off his incredible amount of precious food. Mieka and I almost passed out from shock when we saw this unbelievable hoarding.

This was truly against all principles of human decency. Literally thousands of people were starving to death and here were innumerable bales of grain, dried peas, and dried beans, with scores of smoked sausages and dried hams hanging from the ceiling. To top it all off, Mr. Lummel very proudly showed us three large pickled pigs that he had preserved in large terra cotta pots. There were hundreds of other items, too many to relate. Mr. Lummel also bragged that he had a double set of Ration Cards for his entire family and that the Nazis supplied him weekly with Dutch gin and brandy, and beer. He boasted to us that his salary was so large that he had already saved 3,000 guilders from it. We could not and did not show it then, but Mieka and I were outraged.

When we got back to Mrs. de Graeff's house, and after getting over the shock of this disgusting display of food hoarding while thousands were starving and dying from hunger, we had to contemplate very seriously whether to report them to the Underground. Although Mieka and I were afraid of reprisal, we could not in good conscience stand by and do nothing.

We finally went to Mr. van der Ham, the leader of the Underground, the gentleman who had previously interviewed us, and told him of our experience. He said it sounded unreal, almost like a fairy tale, but already he had visions of giving all those good things to the many starving people the Underground was trying to look after. Then he said the very thing we had feared: "We will need your help." We couldn't very well refuse, now that we had gone this far. We reluctantly promised to cooperate. This involvement could, however, have devastating results for us. It was agreed that a raid would take place during the next new moon. It was winter time and darkness set in very early. The Underground would let us know on exactly which night the raid would take place.

About a week or so later, Mr. van der Ham came to us. "This is it," he said. We were instructed to be at the Lummel's house before curfew time, and to drag our visit out until they arrived. "They" were Mr. van der Ham, who was a professional Dutch Army officer precariously balancing the dual role of officer and Underground leader, and his four confederates, all Underground workers. Mieka and I were told that all of them would be wearing face masks and carrying live weapons. They would treat us in exactly the same manner as the Lummels. The raid would be carried out this way to prevent suspicion on Mr. Lummel's part, who was indeed a very dangerous man with dangerous Nazi connections. We were promised that they would not touch anyone, nor shoot, unless it was unavoidable. In other words, if Mr. Lummel forcibly resisted, then they would shoot.

Naturally, Mieka and I were terrified, and could not even eat the small amount of food allotted to us by the Ration Cards the Underground now regularly supplied us with. Curfew was 8:00 p.m., so at 7:30 p.m. sharp we walked to the other side of the street and rang the Lummels' doorbell. They really liked us very much and were happy to see us. We talked for a while and, though we never touched the stuff, Mr. Lummel served Bols, the famous Dutch gin, loading himself up very nicely. We figured that a tipsy Mr. Lummel wouldn't show too much resistance against five armed, masked intruders. We usually stayed all night, and then afterwards we would sneak back to Mrs. de Graeff's house very carefully, so we wouldn't be caught by the police or the S.S. Mr. Lummel stuck by all the German rules, but apparently he did not see anything wrong with breaking the law of curfew time where it concerned his personal friends. He always wanted us to "stay a little longer."

The conversation was average, sociable, and pleasant, and we dragged it out. Now and then I would glance at the clock, wondering what was taking them so long! It was 9:00 p.m., and so far no one had come! Maybe they decided against it? Just as I relaxed a little, thinking the raid was off, the doorbell rang, startling all of us. The Lummels were just as afraid of the Underground as the Jews were of the Nazis, having near heart attacks each time the doorbell rang, especially at night, knowing it spelled disaster. The Lummels knew very well that during curfew hours the Underground raided the Fascists' homes. The bell startled us too, because we had hoped that those from the Underground had changed their minds.

Mr. Lummel's face grew pale and he refused to go downstairs. Meanwhile, the doorbell kept ringing. Afraid that something might go wrong, I tried to convince him that it wasn't necessarily the Underground, but possibly someone from the airport, and that he was desperately needed for some unexpected duty. The bell rang . . . and rang . . . and kept on ringing, until he finally did go downstairs. Two minutes later, he was back again, but now with his arms way up in the air, followed by a masked man holding a loaded pistol to his neck. Behind them came three more masked, armed men, while the fifth one stood guard downstairs as a lookout for the S.S.

My first impulse, maybe because of nervousness, was to burst out laughing. It all looked so crazy, reminding me of a comedy or a vaudeville act. But I quickly realized the seriousness of it all, and acted according to the instructions Mr. van der Ham, their leader, had given us, namely to act as if we were scared to death.

The masked men told us to stand facing the wall with our hands up, and then they had one man guard us. They grabbed Mr. Lummel, shook him by the shoulders, and demanded that he tell them where the food was hidden. Absolutely petrified, he told them it was upstairs in the attic, and forced into being very cooperative, he showed them the way. In order to avoid any suspicion the Lummels might have about our involvement, Mieka and I were interrogated in the same way as the Lummels. Our captors were rather curt and rough with us too.

The Underground carried off everything, including the eight Ration Cards and the 3,000 guilders Mrs. Lummel had in her pocketbook, as well as the two leather coats the Germans had just given them. Then they shoved the gun in Mr. Lummel's back again, locked him in the bedroom, and shouted that if he ever told the German commander what happened, they would come back and kill him. With that, they stomped out.

As soon as he heard the door slam behind them, Mr. Lummel flew into a rage as he told his wife to unlock his door. He ran into the hall, saw our coats still hanging there, and screamed at us, accusing us of being "in on it" because "they did not take your coats!" The innuendo was that we had betrayed them. This time, we were really scared to death! Thank God I had an answer ready. I told him that it was only logical for them not to take our shabby, old coats, and that it was just as logical that they take the Lummels' brand-new leather ones. He stopped screaming and said, "You have a point there." But all the same, he made it very clear to us that he didn't trust us anymore.

We stayed a little while longer to console them, and then excused ourselves with a "we are very upset and tired," took our leave, and went home. At least that's what we told the Lummels. We did go home, but only for a moment, in case Mr. Lummel was looking through the window, checking on us. Once there, we sneaked out the back door and went straight to Mr. van der Ham's, as he lived only about ten houses away. We knocked out our special code and we were let in. He more or less expected us. We told him it was a terrible mistake that his men did not take our coats too because now the full measure of suspicion was upon Mieka and me. Mr. van der Ham was shocked when we told him how Mr. Lummel had reacted after they left. He had given orders to take the food, Ration Cards, and money, and was not aware that the men, when they saw the coats hanging in the hallway, had grabbed them too. He then asked us if we wanted to stay in his house for the night, just in case Mr. Lummel went to the German commander to file a complaint. Of course, we gladly accepted the invitation.

Very early the next morning, we went back to our house. Taking a few things in our one and only little suitcase, we left for Utrecht. We told Mrs. de Graeff's son, Bob, what happened and he gave us the address of his fiancée in Utrecht. He had called her and she agreed to give us shelter for the time being. There were lots of children in that family, so no beds were available; we slept on the floor.

Three full days passed and we hadn't heard from Bob, so we figured that the coast was clear. It was better for us to go back to Mrs. de Graeff's house because staying away would make the situation appear more suspicious. So Mieka and I walked back to Bilthoven, and I visited the Lummels as soon as we returned. Mieka stayed at home this time, as she was not particularly anxious to see them again.

I rang the Lummels' doorbell and was invited upstairs. When I walked into the living room, I thought I'd die right then and there. A big, tall police officer now confronted me. "Hello," I said, with the most charming of smiles. I really expected the worst. Then, Mrs. Lummel, who had apparently never shared her husband's suspicion of us, said, with an angelic voice, "This is the girl we were just talking about." She announced, very proudly, that I was an opera singer, and that my friend had also been there during the raid.

The policeman interrogated me. Where was I born? Where were my parents? Now I was really glad that Mieka and I had prepared and memorized our new Registration Cards' backgrounds so thoroughly! The policeman even remarked about my lovely little cross (which, as you may recall, was part of my "Italian" identity), so I thanked him very graciously. He then checked my Registration Card and nodded when everything seemed to be in good order. Eventually, he said, he'd like to see my friend too. I told him she was not feeling very well, but that I would go and fetch her. My smile never left my face, yet fear raged like a hurricane within!

When I got home, I told Mieka to go right to bed and pretend that she was very sick. She didn't understand why, but I told her not to ask any questions, just do as I said, "right now!" She undressed quickly and jumped into bed. Then I called the Lummels. I told Mrs. Lummel that Mieka was sick and that she couldn't very well come over because she was in bed. If the policeman insisted, he could visit us where we lived. Mrs. Lummel gave the message to the officer, who answered, "There isn't any hurry. Any time will do." After all, he had already interrogated one witness — me!

I suppose the police left the case hanging because we never heard from them again. Mieka, however, never felt at ease in Bilthoven during the remainder of the war, and was always afraid that something might happen. Just to avoid suspicion, Mieka and I continued to visit the Lummels, but not as frequently as we had. To stop seeing them altogether would certainly have been very unwise and would have created suspicion.

TREE THIEVES

Meanwhile, winter had made her entrance once again, and it was really getting cold. The temperature inside people's houses had become almost unbearable. The only way to get wood to burn, as coal was totally out of the question, was to go to the forest and steal it.

In back of the Lummels' yard, separated by a brook, was a small forest. Most of the trees growing there were silver birch, a kind of wood that dries quickly and burns well. Those trees are usually eighteen to twenty feet tall, and about a foot in diameter. Mieka and I used to go to this forest at night so no one would see us, as the Nazis' law was to "shoot to kill" anyone stealing trees.

With a little handsaw, Mieka and I slaved over a tree until we had it down. It was such an awful job! The saw had only one handle, so we had to switch from time to time, taking turns at the handle and the blade. Like professional lumberjacks, and like "real" thieves, we had to constantly be on the lookout for two things: sawing the tree just enough so that when we pushed it to one side it would fall away from us, and German soldiers on patrol. This forest belonged to the estate the Germans had confiscated for their headquarters! But when people are cold, hungry, and miserable, they are willing to take risks.

After we finally had the tree down, we had to get it home. The shortest route was right through the Lummels' backyard. So, while they were in bed sleeping, that is just what Mieka and I did. We lifted the tree from the ground, Mieka in front, carrying the top part, and me in the back with the trunk. Slowly, we proceeded towards the brook which was about eight feet wide. There we dropped the tree and pushed it so the top of it was resting on the bit of land on the other side.

The job of getting the tree across the brook accomplished, Mieka and I walked as quickly and quietly as possible to the end of the brook, where a little bridge led to our street. From the street, we sneaked back through other people's gardens, like roaming cats, until we finally reached the Lummels' backyard again. In order to get to "our tree," we had to go through their yard and crawl under the barbed wire which separated their garden and the land bordering the brook. Then, with all our might, we pulled the tree across the brook until the greater part of it was on our side in the Lummels' backyard. Once this was accomplished, we considered it a success!

But sometimes the tree we cut was too short, so we could not get enough of it on our side. Others times, the weight of the trunk on the other end was too heavy, and the whole thing slipped out of our hands and plunged into the water, down the brook, and out of sight forever. That happened several times, and it really was heartbreaking. All our efforts were for naught, and since we were freezing, we would have to return to try again. We were persistent, indeed.

Soon we decided that rather than having an easier job of cutting down a smaller tree, we would work harder at the onset and we began to steal taller, bigger trees, all with our one little handsaw. After the entire tree was across the brook, we then pushed its top through the barbed wire, and mustering up all our strength, dragged it into Lummels' yard. From this point on, we took our former positions: Mieka in front and I in the back. Slowly, and oh so quietly, we would steal through Lummels' yard, step by step, until we reached the street. Then, watching and looking to all sides for any sign of danger, we ran as fast as we possibly could with our heavy prey across the street to our house. There we dumped the tree in the backyard for further processing. The next day, we would cut it into appropriate-sized logs for the potbellied stove. After that entire process, we had heat for only one week.

ALMOST CAUGHT

It was raining, and we figured that with such weather, even the Nazis would stay in. We left the house and went to the woods in broad daylight. As usual, we were slaving over "our tree" and had it almost down, when we suddenly spotted a German officer approaching. He was about one hundred yards away, but we could clearly see his uniform. It was like seeing a ghost in the foggy, rainy forest, coming closer and closer. We fell flat on the ground, crawled towards a large heap of leaves, spread handfuls over us for camouflage as quickly as possible, and we waited.

The officer walked towards us, hitting the trees now and then with a little whip he carried. As he came closer, we could hear him softly singing a tune in a low voice. He must have been in a happy mood to be promenading through the woods in the pouring rain, singing.

Now he was no more than ten yards away. What would he do? Shoot us? Arrest us? One thing was certain: If he did not change direction, something was bound to happen. And then, just like a puppet being moved from one spot to another, he walked away from us. It was God's marvelous protection once again.

Mieka and I stayed motionless until the officer was out of sight and then got back to work stealing our tree, as quickly as we could, just in case he returned. Weak from the nervous strain we were under, and exhausted from the job itself, we finally had our tree near the edge of the brook when it slipped out of our hands. Down the bank it went, with a tremendous noise, before it came to rest at the bottom. It layed there as if to defy us, saying, "Come and get me if you can." We were so upset that we both sat down and cried like two little girls who had lost their favorite toy!

The Lummels were never aware of our comings and goings, they never caught us, and I am sure they never ever imagined that we used their garden for our "midnight requisitions." But I'll bet Mr. Lummel would have loved to know, so he could have betrayed us to his boss, the Nazi commander, and maybe get two more leather coats as a reward.

IN "THE LION'S DEN"

It was not long after our cooperation with the Underground's raid on the Lummels' hoarded food that Mieka and I were suddenly visited by Truus, the adoptive mother of Mieka's youngest daughter, Annie. She arrived with the child, and we immediately surmised that something was wrong. Truus knew very well that Mieka was supposed to be single, and that our having the child with us would greatly endanger our position. What could possibly be so serious a matter that she would bring Annie to us?

We found out quickly enough. The Nazis had finally caught up with her husband, Karel. If you recall, Karel was supposedly cooperating with them, but in reality was a leader in the Dutch Underground. They had discovered his real activities, captured him, and now Karel was in jail awaiting execution.

Truus was desperate and on the verge of collapse. What was she to do? She loved both her husband and our Annie with all her heart, but circumstances forced her to part with both of them. Because of the situation with Karel, she felt she needed to safeguard the child. Unable to find another place of protection for Annie so quickly, she brought her back to us. When Truus left us, she was a heartbroken, disconsolate woman. Now, what were we to do?

All this left Mieka and me in a very precarious situation. How were we going to explain this to the Lummels? Everyone would certainly wonder why we suddenly had a child staying with us. Though Annie was blond, she resembled Mieka as far as features were concerned. Mieka and I would have to compose yet another story. Slowly we put the pieces together, and came up with a more-or-less acceptable tale. Since the child still called Mieka "Auntie Katrien," we decided to leave it that way. We would tell our friends and neighbors that Annie was the child of Mieka's sister, who was expecting a baby. Her sister was not feeling too well, therefore she asked Mieka if we could keep Annie with us for a while. This tale was surprisingly well-received by those we were most concerned about — our so-called "friends," the Lummels. From that day on, Annie lived with us.

But the responsibility was now even graver than before. We had to obtain more food, and of course, with a growing child, we would need to buy clothes. That was certainly a problem without textile coupons. Before she left, Truus told us that she had some potatoes for us, and that she wanted us to remove all of Annie's clothing and toys from her house in case the Nazis wanted to inspect their home. Truus had run away with the child, not wanting to lose time in packing Annie's things, but putting her immediate physical protection first.

Mieka asked me to go to Hilversum the next day to pick up the potatoes and the clothes. Little did I know that this would be a trip I would never forget for as long as I lived. I landed in "the lion's den," and only God could get me out.

Before leaving for Hilversum, I went to Mr. van den Ham of the Underground to ask him if he knew where I could get a bicycle. Explaining the situation, he very, very graciously offered his bike because he said it was impossible to get one anywhere else. There was a pair of imitation tires on that bike — solid, airless bands, and non-flexible, just black, hard, round things made of an unknown composition not in the least resembling rubber. They were fixed where rubber tires should normally be, stuffed in between the steel rims. Once on the bike, it felt like I was riding on square wheels. But I gratefully accepted his offer.

The temperature was below zero, and the roads were very icy the day I went to Hilversum. Before leaving, Mieka begged me to take the highway and not to go by way of the "Lage Vuursche," as it would be dangerous to go up and down those small hills. Once I was out of town, I changed my mind and went to the Vuursche anyway. The roads were very treacherous indeed, but I made it.

When I was out of that area, I had to cross through Hilversum, where, during normal times before the war, I broadcasted on a regular basis. The road I had to take passed right by the studios of The Netherlands Broadcasting System! I don't have to tell you how terrified I was of meeting someone I had worked with for so many years from one of the orchestras. Although they loved me and appreciated me then, no one could guarantee that they were not collaborators now!

In my anxiety to avoid them, I went off the specially-designated bicycle path into the middle of the main road. While going as fast as I could to make that "tireless" bicycle move, and turning my head away from the studio side of the street so no one would see my face, I suddenly heard a man's voice shouting "Halt!" My mind, however, was so preoccupied with getting away from the studio, that I didn't realize what was happening until a second "Halt . . . oder wir schiesen!" or, "Stop, or we'll shoot!" got through and I realized the shouting might be meant for me.

Stopping the bicycle immediately, of course, I thought my heart would stop beating too. Two soldiers with bayoneted rifles menacingly marched up to me. My heart was pounding. I felt like a hunted animal. What should I do? Running was suicide, so I just stayed there and did not move.

They asked why I had gone off the bicycle path and onto the

middle of the road. The only answer I could think of was that the other path was too slippery, too icy, and I had already fallen once before, so for safety's sake I had gone into the middle of the road. The soldiers told me to turn around and walk in front of them, their rifles at my back, pointing me towards the entrance of an estate that was now their Gestapo headquarters. They ordered me to tell them my story inside.

I'll never forget how I felt as I walked through that gate. I thought the world had come to an end for me. Now I would surely be deported and murdered. I remember my despair about Mieka and Annie. How would I let them know? What was she to do? She relied so much on me, as she was not a strong person any more, after all the years of fear and persecution we had gone through.

But the two bayoneted soldiers couldn't care less about my feelings. They ordered me to hurry up and tell the officer in charge inside the building about my supposed "violation of the law," their law of course. We walked up a long driveway through gardens, and when we finally came to the entrance of the building, I was met by a Dutch Fascist policeman, a Dutch S.S. He was wearing a Dutch uniform, but with a swastika sewn onto each sleeve. I felt like hitting him right in the face! I was not only terrified, but angry with this collaborator. In my mind, traitors deserved nothing but the worst. He took the bicycle, and then told me to give him my Registration Card! While handing it over, I thanked God for the provision Max had made with the diamonds so that, unlike the experience of my parents being captured because their fingerprints did not match those on their Registration Cards, Mieka and I now had our own fingerprinted cards. The Dutch turncoat then disappeared behind closed doors. After a few minutes, he returned, and told me where to stand and wait until I was called.

Now it was time for my brain to work, and work fast. As the Dutch turncoat walked away, I called him back! I said that I was on a mission for a very sick child, to try to get some food which might possibly save the child's life. I demanded to speak to the commander of this headquarters in person!

I don't know where I had the courage to even think of such a thing, but now I believe, in fact I know, it was God's leading. He gave me that wisdom. The turncoat said he would ask if this could be arranged. Away he went again, and when he returned, the commander was with him, and he told me to come into his office. He tried to express himself in very poor Dutch, and I switched for his convenience to very fine German, much to his surprise. Now the times of hardship I endured with the Theatre of the Prominents, where I had to perform and speak daily with the German artists, paid off. If speaking German did not save my life, it certainly did put this man in a more acquiescent mood.

He questioned me and told me that I should have known that bicycles were not allowed on main roads. It was now or never: I had to use this opportunity to make a logical excuse; I had to try, one way or another, to get out. I gave him my sweetest smile, and then answered him in perfect German. I was very sorry, but coming from another city, I could not possibly have known the rules and regulations of this city, as these stipulations were made locally. He then asked me where I came from, and I told him Bilthoven, twenty-seven miles away, the city of Hilversum, and that the purpose of my trip was to get food and medicine for a friend's sick child.

It wasn't very hard to produce tears as I relayed those circumstances to him. My very life hung in the balance. I was like Daniel in the lion's den. And as with Daniel, God was with me. The Commander inspected the now-infamous "black book" for my Registration Card number but could not find it! God must have blinded his eyes, because my number positively must have been in there! He, however, never saw it! Then he checked my fingerprints. Again, I thank God for the wisdom and for the finances He provided through Max, Mieka's husband, so that when I was caught, my card did have my own fingerprints on it.

Holding my Registration Card in his hand, the Commander now went downstairs with me to look at the bike. I showed him what a piece of junk it really was — all rusted, no tires — and convinced him, with my plight, to give the old, worn out thing back to me. I was positively the best salesperson for the worst bike in the world! I told him that the bike wasn't worth a penny, and that I was more than twenty miles away from home, with no means of getting back if he kept the bike. Smiling, I said, "Sir, I am sure you wouldn't want me to walk all that way?"

He gave me one inquisitive look, abruptly turned to the Dutch turncoat and handed him my Registration Card, then told him to return the bike to me and let me go free. The turncoat returned my card, threw the bike at me, then literally gave me a kick in the bottom and said, "Get out of here! You're really lucky. More than 400 people with bicycles were caught today and not one was given back!" This had obviously been a trap, as the Germans needed all the metal they could get a hold of for their war machine.

Once I was safely outside and on my way, I not only thought, but actually said out loud, "Not only did you return my bike and my Registration Card, but I'm sure I am the only Jew the Gestapo ever let go free!"

THE ACCIDENT

God had so many plans yet for your mother, Felicia. So very many wonderful things were still hidden. But also, so many trying and tragic ones.

Still badly shaken over the arrest, but knowing I had no other choice, for Annie's sake, I continued on my trip to Truus. I wanted to pour my heart out to her, but I was already late in getting the bike back to Mr. van der Ham. So while I relayed a short version of the story, Truus helped me put Annie's clothes and some forty-five pounds of potatoes into a large burlap bag, which we tied to the rack on the back of the bike. When we said goodbye, she tried to smile, but Truus still feared the worst for her husband. As a so-called "traitor," Karel faced execution by a German firing squad. His court case was scheduled to come up in two weeks.

As previously mentioned, the weather was awful, and the roads were treacherous. Because of all that had happened, it was now very late, and Mr. van der Ham had expressly told me that he needed the bicycle back by 4:00 p.m. for Underground use. So I decided, icy or not, I would go over the hilly "Lage Vuursche" to cut time and to try to fulfill my obligation to that truly wonderful patriot. How different he was compared to that Dutch S.S. at Nazi

Gestapo headquarters in Hilversum!

The early part of my trip back over the "Vuursche" went smoothly enough, but just as I was thinking how easy things were going, somehow my bike slipped. The heavy bag with potatoes and clothes pitched to one side, causing the steering wheel to turn towards me. As I plunged to the ground, one of the handlebars cracked my ribs. I was lying there, unable to breathe at first, and in incredible pain, not able to move from under the heavy weight. And then the tears came. My emotions from the whole day's experience finally got the better of me, and I cried my heart out.

A few feet away from me were people stealing trees. They were so anxious to get their own work done, that when they saw me lying on the ground, they just looked and continued to saw down their trees. "Everybody for himself" had become the way of life by our once loving and outgoing population. I sobbed and sobbed. Then God sent help. A man on a bike stopped, bent down over me, and tried to help me up. I became hysterical and let all my pent-up emotions go. I began yelling all kinds of bad things about the Nazis, screaming that they took me prisoner at the Gestapo headquarters earlier that day.

That experience, and my fear, and the terrible pain I was in caused this river of anxiety to overflow. The dam of built-in security, of "secrecy" that we Jews needed to maintain at all times for the preservation of our very lives, had burst! But I just didn't care anymore. However the sweet man put his finger right on my mouth and told me how dangerous it was to say all those things. How fortunate I was that he was against the Germans too. "I could have been a collaborator," he said. I was endangering myself screaming, and he could have made a citizen's arrest right then and there.

He helped me up, tried to comfort me, straightened out my bicycle as much as possible to make it workable, reloaded the burlap bag with potatoes and clothes, and told me to follow him back out of the Lage Vuursche. I climbed on my bike, with intense pain searing my side and chest, and rode behind him all the way back to Hilversum, through the town, to the highway proper. He waved goodbye and disappeared. God's providence, again, was perfect. "Call unto me and I will help." How true is His Word. He sent the "good samaritan" where others did not even care enough to give me a helping hand.

I was faced with a much longer trip back to Bilthoven. It was late — almost 4:00 p.m., and I had hours yet to go. And now a storm had come up. I had twenty-seven miles ahead of me, riding against that storm, in terrible pain complicated by severe breathing problems. Finally, four-and-a-half hours later, I reached Bilthoven. Mieka and Mr. van der Ham had been beside themselves with fear for my life, and they were overjoyed to see me back alive.

It was nearly 8:00 p.m. In spite of the danger of getting caught because of the curfew, and because we knew a woman doctor lived right across the street, Mieka and I went to Merel Lane, our former hideout next to the field of the destroyed antiaircraft batteries. I did not remember her name, but we knew she was reliable. We knocked at her door, and although it was quite late, she let us in. I had several broken and sprained ribs. She taped me up and told me to come back for checkups once a week. It took a full six weeks for me to heal.

As the days passed, we finally heard from Truus. On the very day that Karel was to be executed, Underground forces, clad in German uniform, went into his prison block. One of them, who spoke perfect German and did all the talking, showed falsified documents stating that the guards were to hand over this prisoner. So all of Karel's efforts on behalf of the Jews living in our country were rewarded when the Underground liberated him and hid him until the end of the war.

LIBERATED AT LAST!

The winter brought unbelievable hardships to our people, and many, many died from hunger or lack of medical care. At last, in May, our liberation became a reality. The Germans were defeated on all fronts.

May 5, 1945 we were free, indeed! Free to walk the streets, free to go into stores, free to take a bus, or railroad, or tramway without the dreaded fear of getting caught and deported to a concentration camp. However, it literally took us weeks to adjust to this incredible commodity — freedom. It was quite indescribable. I then understood a little bit about how the Jews must have felt when Moses guided them out of Egypt and into the Promised Land!

The English troops entered Bilthoven. They even helped Mieka in her search for Debora. We went in one of their jeeps to The Hague to Henriette's place. Henriette was there, and we learned what had happened to Simon. He was murdered in a concentration camp, but they had miraculously let her go. Henriette assisted us in tracing Debora's whereabouts, via the Underground, and when we found her, Henriette invited Debora and her "foster parents" to her studio.

The reunion was a strange one, as Debora didn't recognize her own mother. She thought she resembled me, and kept thinking I was her mommy. Debora's foster "mommy" lost her voice completely from the shock that she now had to part with this child, whom she had learned to love as her own. After fourteen years of marriage, that couple had been unable to have children of their own. Since that time, God blessed them because of their love and compassion for this Jewish child and the Jewish people. Shortly after we received Debora back, her foster mother became pregnant herself. God blessed her and her husband not once, but seven times — a perfect number!

Little Annie, who was still with us, had her sister back. They immediately adjusted to each other, as if they had never been separated! Children are so innocent and so flexible!

After ten days in Holland, the English troops were transferred to Germany. Canadian troops took over where the English had left off, helping our Dutch people get back to normal once again.

The first week after the war, Mieka, Annie, Debora, and I moved out of Mrs. de Graeff's house into a lovely home on Cuckoo Lane, owned by a lady who wished to sublet the whole house to us. It was a wonderful place with beautiful furniture and, most importantly, a lovely piano!!

The house was situated close to a school where the Canadian troops were quartered. One day, Debora and Annie pushed their baby doll carriage to the school, to get a closer look at their new "neighbors," the Canadian soldiers. The girls made friends with the army cook. He, in turn, seemed to like the kids, spoiling them with goodies and snacks, of which they had been deprived for so long.

A few days later, just as Mieka and I were getting ready to go to Utrecht, Debora and Annie returned with a Canadian soldier! Debora took matters into her own hands and announced triumphantly, "Mommy, this is the cook who gives us all the good food." The poor fellow was a little embarrassed, but very nice, indeed. We excused ourselves, as we were not able to receive him just then because we were going out, but we asked him if he would like to return that night. He asked us if he could bring a friend with him, and we graciously consented.

THE JOY OF SINGING

At 8:00 p.m. sharp, the cook came and brought the butcher with him. Jan Braun, the restaurant owner in the woods, had lent me his brother's sheet music, and for the first time in all those years, I was really able to sing as much as I wanted to! So when, during the course of our conversation, those two Canadians discovered that I was a singer, they asked me if I would please sing something for them. It all seemed perfectly natural, and I gladly complied.

The soldiers enjoyed every bit of the evening and asked if they could come back. Then they told us that there were two men in their

187

regiment who loved classical music, and they asked if they could bring them along as well. Mieka and I again graciously consented. But what a surprise awaited us that next night! We expected them about the same time, and I remember looking out the window and seeing what appeared to be the entire troop coming towards our house! The cook and the butcher had apparently bragged about us and now everyone wanted to hear this singing "wonder"! It seemed to us as if the whole Canadian Army was on the march and they were all headed for one place — ours! First, there were our two new friends, then two more, and two more, and two more, and so on. On they came, in pairs, rather shyly. I am sure they felt somewhat awkward coming to our house in such great numbers.

When the cook and the butcher entered, they explained what had happened. All the boys had been so anxious to come that they took the liberty of bringing them all along. However, they insisted that if we did not want so many people, we could refuse and they would all march back. But we invited them in. After all, the Dutch government had requested that we be gracious to our liberators and show them hospitality. What better occasion could we offer than to make them all feel welcome.

We needed all the chairs in the house to seat them, and those who could not find a chair took their place on the floor. They were wearing dress uniform, looking their very best, and each one was properly introduced to us by the cook.

MR. SAUNDERS

One of the men introduced to us was Keith Saunders, a tall, very handsome man who was, as I was told, one of the two men who really knew classical music. The other was Michael Smith, a graduate of the University of Jamaica and McGill in Montreal. He was an anthropologist. I learned later that these two "longhaired soldiers," as the others called them, were always in trouble with those who wanted to listen to jazz. To them, it seemed highly unlikely that a cook and a butcher would find an honest-to-goodness opera star in a wee, little town like Bilthoven.

I remember Mr. Saunders sitting in the only rocking chair we had, rocking himself back and forth, asking me, with a polite smile, if I had ever heard of the opera *La Traviatta*. I was not altogether unaware of the sneer in his voice, and I politely answered, "I think so. Do you mean that opera by Verdi?" Then I said that somehow I thought I might remember the melody. He said, "Do you think you could sing some of it? Or possibly just hum a few bars?" I again answered him very politely, "Well. I'm not sure, but I could try . . ."

I had played this opera several times, and had even adopted the name "Violetta de Valerie," the lead role's name, on my Registration Card, as you may recall. Because of all the company we had sitting everywhere on chairs, I decided to be a good sport and sit cross-legged on the floor with those who could not get a seat. I started to sing the first act's famous "e strano" aria, first the recitativo and then the whole aria proper. Never even looking at Mr. Saunders, I sang the entire long aria through to the very end.

The soldiers sat motionless, like little children, and when I was finished, a thundering applause rewarded me. Mr. Saunders sat there with his mouth open. He got up at once, helped me off the floor, shook my hand, and then told me he had been doubtful about the other soldiers' so-called "discovery" but now was extremely happy that he had come along. Michael Smith joined in with him and the requests came one after another. Did I sing this aria and that one? I went to the piano and played and sang for them a while longer. We had tea, and at 10:00 p.m. they all marched off, in twosomes, like good, little boys going back to their boarding school.

The following day brought quite a surprise. Mr. Saunders brought me a large bouquet of roses, along with a record of Brahms' *Fourth Symphony*, which belonged to Michael Smith. Mr. Saunders told me I could keep it as long as I wished. For Mieka and I, who had been deprived of classical music for so long, this was a real treat.

By this time, I was calling Mr. Saunders by his first name, Keith, and he called me Frieda. That night, he asked permission to come back in such a way that I could hardly have refused without being impolite, especially after those beautiful roses. We had some interesting conversations and we began to like each other very much. This went on for several days, and then I asked Mieka for her opinion on whether I should invite Keith for dinner. She told me to go ahead, if I wanted to.

Keith gladly accepted. Mieka and I made as nice a dinner as was possible in those days, and then we all had a lovely, quiet time with a little music afterwards. Later on that evening, Mieka said that she was awfully tired, and excused herself to go to bed. I told her I would follow in a little while.

Keith and I were now left alone, and the conversation went in a totally different direction. He suddenly took me in his arms, and right then and there proposed to me. I was so surprised, I didn't know quite what to answer. He told me of his love for me, and I gave him my answer — "yes" — much to my own amazement.

I ran up the stairs and got Mieka out of bed, who was so sleepy she could hardly keep her eyes open. I asked her to come down right away because we had something important to tell her. In those days, we were still deprived of electricity, so we were using candles given to us by the Canadians. Keith and I had been talking by candlelight, which made for quite a romantic atmosphere.

Now Mieka came downstairs in her light blue dressing gown, carrying a lighted candle, looking for all the world like Florence Nightingale. We asked her to sit down and listen to what Keith had to say. I expected Mieka to be amazed, even surprised. But how can I describe her reaction? Keith told her rather formally that he had asked me to become his wife. Mieka jumped up as if a bee had stung her. "What!" she said, "Marry her? I think you both have gone crazy!" She told him to get out, and fast, and go back to his "school" (which was their headquarters). But she meant it literally, as if he were a child she could send away! And to me she simply said, "And you! You get upstairs and go to bed!" It was just as if my mother had suddenly returned and was giving me a lesson on "how to behave."

Poor Keith left, a very unhappy man, and I obediently went to bed. As you may know, once a man is in love, there is no stopping him. Of course, Felicia, there was no stopping your father either. The very next morning, under some "made-up" pretense, Keith returned with another armful of dozens of roses, telling me that his proposal of the night before was still valid, and asking me if my "yes" was still valid too. By now I had really fallen in love with him, so I reaffirmed my "yes" with a kiss.

We informed Mieka of our decision. She could not get over it. Later on, we went to the offices of the local newspapers and the Utrecht daily newspapers, announcing our engagement to be married. We had to wait, however, for the permission of the general, as all war brides had to be cleared first, with information gathered as to whether I had been loyal to the Allies during the war. I was interrogated by army officials and an army chaplain, and finally, after waiting from the end of May until October, we received permission to be married. Since Debora had more or less been the spark of our first meeting, we decided that we would be married on her birthday, November 8.

"SOMETHING BORROWED, SOMETHING BLUE"

So, on November 8, 1945, Keith Saunders and Frieda van Hessen were married. There was never a wedding like ours, I am sure, in all of history. After all the years of running and hiding, the last thing I had was clothes to wear, and certainly not proper wedding attire! The only thing left to do was to borrow my wedding apparel. Clothing, however, along with all the necessities of life, was very hard to come by, and wedding gowns were like something out of a fairy tale. They were a beautiful memory, like something that existed only in days gone by. Unfortunately, at this time, they did not exist.

I did the next best thing: I made the rounds of my acquaintances. From one friend I borrowed a suit, from another a blouse, from a third a pair of shoes, and so on.

When a person from Bilthoven gets married, the couple can only get married in The Bilt, the next town, as Bilthoven resides under the township of The Bilt. The wedding was to be at 11:00 a.m. but there were no vehicles. The Bilt is ten miles away, and it is rather hard for a bride and groom to walk all that way. So, my husband-to-be thought of something much better: He borrowed an Army truck for the occasion. Giving the driver cigarettes for his kindness, and putting up empty orange crates for seats, Keith drove up in front of the house at 7:00 in the morning! He was so excited about his last-minute truck arrangement that he couldn't wait any longer. He had to come right away to show us! He also had to be back with the truck before anyone found out, to keep the originally-assigned driver out of trouble. We shared some coffee and breakfast, and then I went back into the bedroom to prepare for the great event.

Everything was the way it was supposed to be, including "something borrowed, something blue." The suit was blue, and nearly everything else I wore was borrowed! The only exception was the one evening gown I had somehow managed to keep with me all through the war. This gown I intended to wear at the reception.

When 10:00 a.m. arrived, it began to rain. By 10:30 it rained even harder. But when 10:45 came along, and we had to leave, it poured! The rain came down in buckets. "Here comes the bride . . . " running from the house to the truck, followed by faithful friends and the few relatives who had survived the war. All of us were running like chicks to the coop, to get into the truck as quickly as we could, and off we went to the wedding. Because of all the commotion, we were late in leaving, but now we were finally on our way, everybody wet, sitting in the most dignified way they could on orange crates.

We arrived at The Bilt's Town Hall exactly twenty minutes late. My mother had always told me that I would be late for my own wedding, as it always took me so long to get dressed, and her prediction, indeed, came true. By the time we arrived, the mayor, annoyed with our delay, had left, and had given his assistant charge to marry us. The ceremony itself was simple, but because we were married in Dutch and in English, the whole process became awfully complicated. All I can remember is saying "Yes" and "I do" I don't know how many times, until finally I gathered that we were really married, because Keith gave me "the kiss" that usually means you are now husband and wife. The double language ceremony had been quite confusing to me, as my knowledge of English left much to be desired in those days. From Town Hall we all went back to the house, where everyone gathered downstairs and waited for me to get changed into my one and only salvaged evening gown.

THE MAPLE LEAF CLUB

Because my parents had been put to death for being Jewish, and Keith's parents were in Montreal, the army had arranged a wedding reception for us in the Canadian Maple Leaf Club in Hilversum. We invited Truus and Karel, Henriette and Sixta, who was the late Simon's assistant and had become a dear friend to us. Steve Bardega, an Army friend of Keith's, and his wife were also there.

And from my family: Uncle Koos and his wife, Ans; my brother Bernard, and his wife, Daisy; Mieka and her sister, Andrea.

At the Maple Leaf Club, we were ushered into a lovely, very large room where a small orchestra was playing. We were showered not only with kindness, but with the most exquisite food we had seen in years. Of course, there was a beautiful wedding cake, photographers from the local papers, the Canadian papers, and not to forget, the army newspaper.

There was wine and rejoicing, and all that goes with a wedding. But the most fantastic thing of all I realized over half a year after the wedding took place. Waking up one night, being pregnant with you, Felicia, it suddenly struck me that our wedding had been held in the same building where, a year before, I had been taken as a captive and almost deported to a concentration camp. The Maple Leaf Club was in the same building that had formerly housed Gestapo headquarters!

God works His wonders to perform, indeed, in the most unusual ways. But He had yet to perform a greater wonder.

THE SEED

For our honeymoon, Keith and I went to The Hague. We stayed for one week in Henriette's studio apartment, which she had graciously offered to us while she went to stay with a friend. We had a quiet, very lovely honeymoon, and made all kinds of plans for our future. All the while I wondered what it would be like to live in another country so far away, and where I would hear nothing but English all day long.

My English was not very good then, as I said, and I was having immeasurable difficulty pronouncing "th" as this consonant combination does not exist in the Dutch language. To be honest, I was not particularly looking forward to having to speak English either. However, wedding vows constitute that the wife shall follow her husband wherever he goes, and there was not much choice left but to go with him to Canada. I would have to wait a while, though. Many, many war brides had married before I took this step and they were all waiting for their turn to get free transportation over the ocean to their new homeland.

I resumed my singing career, and was singing concerts and broadcasts again. I was very content to be back at it. Towards the end of January, Keith received notice that he had to go back to Canada some time in February. We had not anticipated this, and now I would have to wait all alone. No one knew, not even the Canadian Embassy, when I would get my turn to follow. They said it could be as long as a year.

We told Bernard and Daisy about Keith's scheduled departure. They kindly invited us to stay with them for a last reunion and were the most gracious hosts in their newly-acquired home. While there, my Uncle Koos, my father's younger brother and the only one left on my father's side of my family because he had a Gentile wife, paid us a visit. He invited us for a week's stay with him and his family in Amsterdam. We accepted gladly, happy that Keith would have a chance to get to know them better before leaving for Canada.

Keith was awfully lucky as far as weekend passes were concerned, and had the most wonderful cooperation from his fellow officers. They all liked him and were sorry that he had to leave his wife behind. To make it a little easier on him, they made it easier for him to get passes. So Keith and I left for Amsterdam for our week's stay at my Uncle Koos and Aunt Ans' in their positively beautiful home.

The first few days were, of course, taken up by our getting to know one another and, quite naturally, by Koos and Ans hearing some of my war experiences. My uncle suggested that I write a book, for posterity, so my children would know what their mother went through. While listening to the incredible events of my story, my uncle had an idea. He advised me to "become a Christian" as soon as possible. He maintained that as soon as I would set foot in Canada, I would have to fill out papers, and if there were ever another war, I might have to go through the same persecution again. Ans was Protestant, and it was, as I said before, because of the fact that my uncle was married to a non-Jew that he and their two boys had escaped the Holocaust. Jews who had married Gentiles and children of those marriages were not deported to concentration camps, but still had to wear the hated yellow star as a "warning" that Gentiles should not mix with them.

My first reaction was one of sheer perplexity. I was dumbfounded and couldn't believe I had heard him correctly. Koos argued it was the only wise thing to do. I told him my parents were put to death because they were Jewish, and it would be impossible for me to ever deny that I was Jewish-born. I said I intended to die Jewish, or else Hitler had won the war after all. Keith agreed, saying he fell in love with a Jewish girl and married a Jewish woman, and that only if I had the true desire to do so should I become "a Christian." Nothing more was said about it any more during our stay, and we continued to have a wonderful time.

But, as I have said before, God's ways are not our ways. Now I am convinced that He used my Uncle Koos' worldly attitude to plant "the Seed of Life" in my heart.

The time of Keith's departure was drawing near, and he only had a few days left in Holland. I suddenly asked him, "Do you think I should change?" "Change what?" Keith asked. I said, "My religion — before I come to Canada." He was surprised to find me still thinking about this, and told me that if I wanted to, I would have to make the decision myself. I promptly asked him to come with me to see Mr. Frank, the Protestant minister of the Dutch Reformed Church in Bilthoven. Keith agreed. When we rang the bell, a maid opened the door. Mr. Frank was out visiting the sick. I asked her when he would be back, and she made an appointment for us for the following day. I knew that Keith would not be there, but decided to accept that time anyway, as I realized that in the end, it was to be my decision and not Keith's.

The next day I was welcomed by Mr. Frank, a very nice, older gentleman, who asked, "How can I help you?" I told him about the discussion with my uncle, my future, and my husband's opinion, and abruptly requested to "become a Christian." During the war, most ministers would give a "certificate of Christian faith" to any Jewish person requesting one. But now it was a different story. Mr. Frank told me I should bear in mind that the war was over, and that he could no longer comply with people's requests for certificates without them knowing the Gospel. He then asked me what I knew about Jesus. I told him what I knew about His life, remembering all the paintings I had seen in the Catholic Church while I was dating Kees, and that I realized how Jesus had suffered. After all, I wanted to make a good impression.

And then, unexpectedly, something happened. Up to this point, Mr. Frank had listened very politely to me, but now he got up from his chair, stood right in front of me, and while looking straight into my eyes, said, "How much do you believe of what you have just told me?" It was then that, as it were, a Hand was laid over my mouth, God's Hand, preventing me from telling a lie. I looked up at him and said, with great humility, "Nothing."

Mr. Frank put his arm very gently around my shoulder, and asked if I wished to look into Christianity and study it for a while to see if I could accept it. I nodded, and after a quiet cup of tea with him, I agreed to study with a lady who knew both Judaism and Christianity. Her name was Elizabeth, and God showed me how wrong it is to judge people by their nationality, as sweet Elizabeth was a German-born lady.

In her early years, "Liza" had married a Dutch Orthodox Jewish man, the eldest son of a Jewish family, where she had been hired as a governess. She had accepted the Jewish faith and had lived for thirty-three years as an Orthodox Jew. Then, during our most horrible wartime experiences, her husband died suddenly of a heart attack, leaving her inconsolable. She could not stop grieving. Elizabeth barely existed, having given up on life. Then, one balmy summer's night while Liza was sitting in an unlit room and staring into a moonlit firmament, the Lord Himself appeared to her. She told me that she saw just the outline of His Person, and then His two beautiful large eyes, like two pools of love and compassion, as He spoke to her. He said, "Elizabeth, fear not. Do not grieve any longer. Read My Word. Begin with Job." And then He left, leaving her awestruck, marveling at such love.

Following her experience, Liza could more clearly comprehend what Mary must have felt during the annunciation. Instantly Liza was changed. She now knew that Jesus was indeed the Messiah, the One she had known when she was a teenager in Germany, and later rejected for thirty-three years as an Orthodox Jew. She gladly accepted Him as her Lord, and became His faithful servant. Elizabeth had the most wonderful, real conversion, and although still saddened by her husband's death, she felt a certain peace and a contentment that "passed all understanding."

The pastor, Mr. Frank, told her about my request, and he suggested to her that she might want to teach me. She gladly consented, and God sent her as a teacher into my life. I told Keith about my decision. He again said that it was all up to me, and that he would never force me to change my religion.

One week later, Keith returned to Canada while I patiently awaited my turn with the other "war brides." He was very sad because of our separation but hoped that it would not be for too long. Another week had gone by and I started my first lesson with Elizabeth. Our first discussion was the prologue to an incredible mental and spiritual battle. We started reading the Gospel of John. But each time we read the New Testament, I became more upset. Telling her that I was an intellectual, and I thought that she was too, how then could she believe all these "fairy tales?" This went on for five weeks. I truly thought she had lost it!

My mental and spiritual opposition just would not leave, nor would I give in. Poor Elizabeth had an awful time of it. She pondered how to approach this problem. Then, when Liza came back the sixth week, she told me she had not been sent to fight and argue with me, but to teach me about Jesus. She said she would come back only one more time, the seventh week, and she now had only one request: that I would please read Isaiah 53 and the 22nd Psalm by David this week. I agreed.

Six days went by, and I could no longer procrastinate. I went to a small room in the house, closed the door, and opened up the Bible. Finally finding the Book of Isaiah, I began to read, but I did not comprehend a word. Liza told me to read it, so I read. I had become rebellious, and Satan was bombarding this last vestige.

But God, in His wisdom, had said to Elizabeth, "Tell her to read Psalm 22." And that's when Satan lost. I finished Isaiah 53, like I said, not understanding a word, and looked for Psalm 22. I found it, and what did I see: "My God, my God, why hast Thou forsaken me?" I mentioned before that I was a professional soprano, and remembered that in Bach's "St. Matthew's Passion," the basso, portraying the Lord, sings, "My God, my God, why hast Thou forsaken me?" Still in my rebellion, I said, "What do you know, they stole this from Bach!"

Oh, God is so wise! This finally got my attention. Now I wanted to continue reading to see what else had been "stolen" from Bach! Then I came to verse 16, and read "They pierced my hands and my feet." Almost in shock, I literally yelled out "That's Jesus!" Mercifully, I had never known that thousands had been crucified, but I knew that Jesus died in that devastating way. The Jews stoned people to death but did not crucify them. Crucifixion was a Roman death penalty. Yet David wrote Psalm 22, prophesying this form of death hundreds of years before crucifixion was ever invented and practiced by the Romans.

Now I was perplexed, and said, "How could I have lived all these years without knowing this? It's like coming out of a dark hole into the light." And I never even knew that Jesus called Himself "The Light of the World." Then I reread Isaiah 53, and clearly understood that it described the whole crucifixion and resurrection of Jesus. Instantly, God had taken the blinders off my eyes and Satan was defeated! I called Elizabeth, who came over immediately, and together we read Isaiah 53. Then, all of it became very clear to me: how "He was despised and rejected of men," how He was a "man of sorrows and acquainted with grief," how "we hid our faces from Him," how "He had been afflicted and wounded for our transgressions," and how "with His stripes we are healed." I realized how "all of us, like sheep, have gone astray," and how "He died for our iniquities." Yes, for my sins too.

I reasoned that if David, 1,444 years BC, and Isaiah, 762 years BC, both knew Him, and Paul, a Pharisee, saw Him and knew Him, then I needed no further proof. I accepted Him too, as my Lord and Savior. Elizabeth told me how she had prayed for my enlightenment, and how she had despaired about my inability to listen. God says, "Be still and know that I am God." The whole time I was saying, "I won't be still, and I won't listen!" I can only appreciate how Elizabeth never forced anything upon me, but left it all between God and me, leaving it entirely up to Him to work out His plan of salvation.

Now came the weeks of happiness, the joy of reading this wonderful Book we call the Word of God. With my acceptance of God's truth, it seemed that my inability to understand the language suddenly disappeared. I wondered how it had been possible that I could not understand it before. It was as clear as daylight, and now I know that God, because of Israel's disbelief, said that He would make them "seeing blind" and "hearing deaf" but "for a remnant," and that I belong to this remnant. Hallelujah!

I studied very hard, and in a few months I went to see the minister and asked him to accept me into his congregation. I came before the Board of Elders and told them what I believed and knew to be the truth. I had previously given my testimony in a private session to Mr. Frank. It was then decided that I should be baptized. During a wonderful Sunday morning service in May, I was baptized and accepted as a member of the Dutch Reformed Church, thereby becoming a true member of the body of Christ, and not, as I had first intended it, "a Christian" in name only.

I realized that through the war, God had been with me, and that now, at last, I knew Him. I believe that He indeed gave His only begotten Son, that "whosoever believeth on Him shall not perish, but have everlasting life." "God is not a man that he should lie" as indeed He had preserved me all these years for Himself.

On June 4, 1946, I sailed for the "New World" and into a new marriage as a war bride. I was blessed with a brand-new faith in God, and a new understanding of that book, the Word of God, as the man dressed in black in Germany had called it when he begged me to read it before the Holocaust. After all that has happened and through all these many years, this glorious book has become my companion — my familiar friend.

EPILOGUE

After the war, I did go back to the old house. There was only a heap of stones left, as it had been ransacked for its wood and for what was left of our belongings. That is the past. But now, look at how God has replenished me through the years, and blessed my then-unknown future, loving me for who I am.

Many years have come and gone since my sailing for the New World in 1946. You, dear Felicia, are now yourself a mother of two adult daughters, Erika and Cassandra.

I am now in the winter of my life, and in retrospect, I can tell you that in the midst of my storms, my wildernesses, and my joys — which were many — God has preserved me all these years. He was, is, and always will be there.

And although I did not know Him then, now I know His Name — Yeshua Ha Mashiach — Jesus, the Messiah!

AFTER THE WAR:
History & Answers to the Eleven Most Often Asked Questions

1. *What is your birthdate and place of birth?*

I was born Frieda Ella van Hessen on April 24, 1915 in Amsterdam, The Netherlands.

2. *What are your parents' names? Do you have any memories of how they interacted with each other, and with you and your brothers?*

My parents were Izak van Hessen (father) and Sarlina Diamant (mother). We had a very close family life, held together by love and our combined interest in music, art, and sports.

3. *What are your memories of your mother?*

My mother had a beautiful soprano voice, which she inherited from her father, who had a wonderful baritone voice, and who was a member of the then-famous Apollo Choir, partaking in many of their performances. My mom studied with Anton Averkamp, then a reknowned voice teacher. She did not perform in any concert, but I remember, among others, her singing at home the aria "Erbarme dich mein God" (have pity on me, my God) from the *Saint Matthew Passion* by Bach, and the aria of "Salome of Herodiade" by Massenet, accompanied by my older brother, Bernard, who was a fine and accomplished pianist.

4. How did your career end?

As destiny would have it, in my own career before the Nazi disaster ended it, I was the soloist at a concert of the Apollo Choir in the Amsterdam Concertgebouw, the Dutch equivalent of Carnegie Hall in New York. There I performed and was accompanied at the piano by my fiancé, Anton Dresden, son of Sam Dresden, who was the Director of the Conservatoire of Music in Amsterdam.

The next day, the review consisted of only one sentence: "Because the soloist is a Jew, and after all the suffering we have done already because of the Jews, I feel not called to review her performance . . . " That then became my last official concert performance in Holland.

A while later, my fiancé was told by his parents to end our engagement. He was half Jewish, and they thought that by marrying me he would be considered full Jewish. I was told in no uncertain terms by a niece in his family, whom I met in a private room in their home, that they would send the police after me if I did not comply! Needless to say, in the midst of the raging war, and fearing for my very life most of the time, this left me brokenhearted.

5. *What was your father's occupation?*

I adored my dad. Being the only girl between two boys, I was "his little girl." He was a businessman and in the Reserve, a Captain of the Corps of Engineers with the army. During the Dutch mobilization he was asked to become a full-time officer.

6. *What memories do you have of your grandparents?*

My grandparents were Vrouwtje and Eliezar Diamant. My grandmother's sister was married to Abraham Ascher, owner of the largest diamond factory in Western Europe at the time. He was a very prominent figure in Holland and very much involved with charities. He and his family all perished in the war. I just loved visiting my grandma. The house they lived in had an annex leading down to the kitchen by a small, unpainted, wooden staircase. When I arrived for a day's visit, she knew how to entertain me! She handed me a pail with soapy water and a big brush and I could scrub that staircase as much and as long as I wanted! Then at lunchtime, we sat down at her table, and before I was allowed to eat, she closed her eyes and said a prayer in Hebrew, which she tried at length to make me repeat. Once I asked her what that all meant and she told me that she did not know, but it was the "broche" (prayer) one was supposed to say before eating bread!

7. What memories do you have of your other relatives?

Esther was my mom's much beloved niece, who spent most Sundays at our home. She was in hiding with my parents and perished with them after being deported to Auschwitz.

My dad's oldest brother, Heyman, was what we in Holland called a "gentleman farmer" because instead of working the land himself, he had servants who provided the labor. He lived in gorgeous farmhouse along the river Amstel, outside of Amsterdam, where I loved to visit and where I learned a lot about farming — like milking cows and other things that made for an exciting outing for a youngster. He perished at Bergan Belsen as did his young son, Bernard, and Bernard's wife, Clara, at another camp. Heyman's wife was fortunate in a way; she had died a natural death before all this happened.

Another of my dad's brothers, Riko, had an office in Amsterdam. One day his son, Bob, had returned from lunch and was walking up the stairs to the office when he was met by two Nazis. They questioned him, asking who he was. After he told them, they informed him that his father had just died what they called "a hero's death," because he had refused to go with them to Gestapo headquarters. Running upstairs, Bob found his father dead, just as they had said, slumped over his desk.

My Aunt Rosa, my father's only sister, and her eighty-seven-year-old husband, were dragged out of their house by the Nazis. Both perished in Auschwitz, and as described in my story, so did my sweet kid brother, Eddie, betrayed by his lawyer at age twenty-nine. My father and mother, of course, also perished in Auschwitz.

Most of our friends and acquaintances were killed, leaving me with my brother, Bernard, and my Uncle Koos (nickname for Jacob in Dutch), who was my father's youngest brother (he was married to a Gentile lady, Ans Diecke), and my Uncle Sally, the next to the youngest of my dad's brothers. Uncle Sally lived in Paris, where his Gentile girlfriend protected him and he survived.

My brother, Bernard, had worked with the Underground while in hiding, for which the American government awarded him the Medal of Honor and citizenship for helping two American pilots escape when their plane went down. Six years older than I, Bernard was a wonderful, loving, protecting, and helpful brother. He died in 1980.

Before the war, I, and my brothers — Bernard, my older brother, and Eddie, my younger brother — gave many live concerts together, both broadcasting and at the very "cool" events of those days, called Home Concerts. Our home was big enough to seat some thirty-five to forty people, whom we entertained with piano and violin sonatas, trios of violin, piano, and violincello, played at that time by my then fiancé, Anton Dresden, and of course by my singing repertoire. These were wonderful events, indeed.

8. Was your family completely nonreligious?

As for religious education, there was none for me, but

my brothers had bar mitzvahs and both married in the synagogue. As a six-year-old child, when I asked why I had to stay home from school because of Grote Verzoendag (the Day of Atonement), it was explained to me that it was just another holiday. Christianity was never mentioned in our home either. Except for my brothers' bar mitzvahs, no pork, and no Gentile boyfriend being allowed, my siblings and I were brought up without God in our lives. However, we were very Jewish and we did have matzos each year (though I never knew why) except that it was always at Easter time, never having been told about Passover. I didn't even know anything about Moses until I became a Christian!

9. Is Sinterklaas a religious holiday?

Sinterklaas is not a religious event, but nearly everybody celebrates it, except for perhaps Orthodox Jews who celebrate Chanukah. But then, I did not associate with any Orthodox Jews, so at that time I was not aware of religious happenings.

10. What happened to your home in Amsterdam and did you ever go back there?

We lived at 121 Nieuwe Herengracht, in Amsterdam. It was a big home, built in the eighteenth century in the so-called "Golden Age" for Holland, due to their posession of the East and West Indies. In those early days, that home consisted of some forty rooms, which were later converted into three large apartments. We lived at the top floor, and that included the very large attic, converted by us into guest rooms, while the first floor apartment included a full basement.

During the war, our home was ransacked for wood to be used for heating. People knew that all of the three-story inhabitants were taken away or had left. The house was turned into ruins, with the stones left on a flat boat in the canal. When I went back some time after the war to see where I had lived my beautiful, carefree, and blessed life, there was a big, gaping hole instead of our building. Looking up, I saw the wallpaper from my bedroom on the retaining wall of the next building, reminding me of my "golden days" in that once-so-cherished home . . . I nearly collapsed at the sight.

In the 1980s, I returned a second time to Amsterdam and saw that where our big home once stood, two houses had been built, leaving me with just the memories. I looked over at the other side of the canal and saw lovely Wertheim Park, named after a famous philantropic Jew! Its gorgeous trees had not changed over the years. I remembered the wonderful view from our three-story high apartment, the rain pelting against our big windows, looking out at that park as I was wont to do. Even now, it was still there, and it was still beautiful . . . I realized that people may negatively change things, but God never does.

11. What happened to Mieka and her children?

They emigrated to the United States. Mieka became a

pediatric nurse, Debora became a fashion model, and Annie became a very successful businesswoman.

THE DEAD SEA SCROLLS
ISAIAH 53

Isaiah's prophecy of a suffering Messiah
(approximately 760 BC, confirmed in the find of the Dead Sea Scrolls)

¹ Who hath believed our report? and to whom is the arm of the LORD revealed?
² For he shall grow up before him as a tender plant, and as a root out of a dry ground: he hath no form nor comeliness; and when we shall see him, there is no beauty that we should desire him.
³ He is despised and rejected of men; a man of sorrows, and acquainted with grief: and we hid as it were our faces from him; he was despised, and we esteemed him not.
⁴ Surely he hath borne our griefs, and carried our sorrows: yet we did esteem him stricken, smitten of God, and afflicted.
⁵ But he was wounded for our transgressions, he was bruised for our iniquities: the chastisement of our peace was upon him; and with his stripes we are healed.
⁶ All we like sheep have gone astray; we have turned every one to his own way; and the LORD hath laid on him the iniquity of us all.
⁷ He was oppressed, and he was afflicted,

yet he opened not his mouth: he is brought as a lamb to the slaughter, and as a sheep before her shearers is dumb, so he openeth not his mouth.

[8] He was taken from prison and from judgment: and who shall declare his generation? for he was cut off out of the land of the living: for the transgression of my people was he stricken.

[9] And he made his grave with the wicked, and with the rich in his death; because he had done no violence, neither was any deceit in his mouth.

[10] Yet it pleased the LORD to bruise him; he hath put him to grief: when thou shalt make his soul an offering for sin, he shall see his seed, he shall prolong his days, and the pleasure of the LORD shall prosper in his hand.

[11] He shall see of the travail of his soul, and shall be satisfied: by his knowledge shall my righteous servant justify many; for he shall bear their iniquities.

[12] Therefore will I divide him a portion with the great, and he shall divide the spoil with the strong; because he hath poured out his soul unto death: and he was numbered with the transgressors; and he bare the sin of many, and made intercession for the transgressors.

PROPHECY WRITTEN IN 1444 BC
PSALM 22

Fifth Messianic Psalm:
Christ's suffering and coming glory

[1] My God, my God, why hast thou forsaken me? Why art thou so far from helping me, and from the words of my roaring?

[2] O my God, I cry in the daytime, but thou hearest not; and in the night season, and am not silent.

[3] But thou art holy, O thou that inhabitest the praises of Israel.

[4] Our fathers trusted in thee: they trusted, and thou didst deliver them.

[5] They cried unto thee, and were delivered: they trusted in thee, and were not confounded.

[6] But I am a worm, and no man; a reproach of men, and despised of the people.

[7] All they that see me laugh me to scorn: they shoot out the lip, they shake the head, saying,

[8] He trusted on the LORD that he would deliver him: let him deliver him, seeing he delighted in him.

[9] But thou art he that took me out of the womb: thou didst make me hope when I was upon my mother's breasts.

[10] I was cast upon thee from the womb: thou

art my God from my mother's belly.

[11] Be not far from me; for trouble is near; for there is none to help.

[12] Many bulls have compassed me: strong bulls of Bashan have beset me round.

[13] They gaped upon me with their mouths, as a ravening and a roaring lion.

[14] I am poured out like water, and all my bones are out of joint: my heart is like wax; it is melted in the midst of my bowels.

[15] My strength is dried up like a potsherd; and my tongue cleaveth to my jaws; and thou hast brought me into the dust of death.

[16] For dogs have compassed me: the assembly of the wicked have inclosed me: **they pierced my hands and my feet.**

ABOUT THE AUTHOR:
Frieda Roos - van Hessen

Frieda van Hessen was named one of the world's top opera and concert singers. At nineteen, she sang the lead for the Dutch version of Walt Disney's *Snow White*. At twenty-one, Van Hessen was awarded the Grande Diplome at the World Contest in Geneva, Switzerland where judges said she was one of the eight best female singers in the world. At twenty-four, she was the soloist in a performance of Verdi's *Requiem* for the Dutch Royal Family. Unfortunately, World War II cut short Frieda van Hessen's career, singing her last performance in the Amsterdam Concertgebouw, the Dutch equivalent of Carnegie Hall in New York.

Since the war, Frieda van Hessen has immigrated to the United States and now lives in North Carolina. At over ninety years old, she spends her time doing needlework, painting, and serving the Lord.

Also Available from
HARVEST DAY BOOKS

$15.95

Jungle Jewels & Jaguars
Living with the Amueshas Translating God's Word
By Martha Tripp

The true story of a young woman's journey deep into the jungles of Peru to live with the native Amuesha tribe, learn their language, and bring to them the Word of God in their native tongue. This amazing memoir brings us the trials and triumphs of 23-year Bible translation mission.

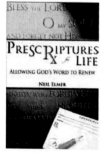

$15.95

Prescriptures for Life
Allowing God's Word to Renew
By Neil Elmer

Prescriptures for Life is about tapping into God's power to overcome obstacles that get in the way of moving forward in life. This user -friendly book provides pertinent Scripture in a topical format — easy to use and share with a friend.

Order at www.ReadingUp.com

Harvest
Day
Books

$12.95

Together We Can!

A Mosaic of Stories and Devotions Displaying the Impact of God's Word

By Aretta Loving

"Together We Can! brings us stories about the truth of God's Word, changed lives, miracles, and increased faith. The one thing they all have in common is the power of the Word of God … "

- Dr. John R. Watters,
Exec. Dir. Wycliffe International

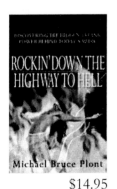

$14.95

Rockin' Down the Highway to Hell

Discovering the Hidden Satanic Power Behind Today's Music

By Michael Plont

Exposes the perils, snares, and hidden satanic power of the rock music culture. This book is a real eye-opener for high schoolers, parents, teachers, coaches, and anyone concerned about our youth and young adults.

Order at www.ReadingUp.com

ORDER FORM

For additional copies of Life in the Shadow of the Swastika, *or for any Harvest Day book, please fill out the following information or visit our web site at* www.ReadingUp.com. *Discounts are available for bulk orders and to bookstores and libraries.*

Fax orders: (231)929-1993
Telephone orders: (231)929-1999
Email orders: Orders@BookMarketingSolutions.com
Postal orders: BMS
                           10300 Leelanau Court
                           Traverse City, MI 49684

•••

Please send the following Books: I understand that I may return any of them for a full refund–for any reason, no questions asked.

_____

_____

_____

Name: _____
Address: _____
City: _____ State: _____ Zip: _____ – _____
E-mail address: _____

Sales Tax: Please add 6% for products being shipped to Michigan addresses.
Shipping by air
          US: $4.50 for the first book, $0.50 for each additional book.
          International: $9.00 for the first book, $5.00 for each additional
          book (estimate)

Payment: ☐ Check   ☐ Credit Card:
☐ Visa   ☐ AMEX   ☐ MasterCard   ☐ Discover

Card Number: _____
Name on Card:_____ Exp. Date: ____ / _____